Well-Heeled

THE REMARKABLE STORY OF

The Public Benefit Boot Company

Well-Heeled

THE REMARKABLE STORY OF
The Public Benefit
Boot Company

Brian Seddon & David L. Bean

PHILLIMORE

2004

Published by
PHILLIMORE & CO. LTD
Shopwyke Manor Barn, Chichester, West Sussex, England

ISBN 1 86077 313 3

Printed and bound in Great Britain by
CAMBRIDGE PRINTING

For two very special girls –

Annie and Babs

Contents

Acknowledgements

Many people and organisations assisted in the preparation of this book. The authors wish to thank them all, especially the following:

The Franklin family and in particular the late Clifford Franklin, who provided much of the initial inspiration for this book;

Paul Gibson for invaluable help, patient proofreading, on-going encouragement and kind permission to use photos from his collection;

Arthur Hudson, former manager of the Leeds Benefit Footwear repair facility, for helpful advice and the use of photos;

Christopher Ketchell, Local History Unit, Hull College, for continued encouragement, assistance and use of photos.

Particular thanks are also extended to the following individuals and organisations for their very kind encouragement and assistance:

Ray Barlow (Accrington and Rossendale College, Lancashire); Anthony Bean; Andrew Bolt; the late Tilly Brennan; the late Bernard Brown; Betty Brown; Alan Clark; Sue Constable (Shoe Collection, Northampton Borough Council); Maxwell Craven (former Keeper of Antiquities, City of Derby); David Edwards (Flambards Village, Helston, Cornwall); Douglas R. P. Ferriday; John Gilleghan MBE; Ann Krawszik (Chesterfield Library); Tony Mackrill; Allan and Judy Marshall; Andrew McKay (Keeper, Shoe Collection, Northampton Borough Council); John Morgan; Bruce Robinson (former Assistant Managing Director BSC); Rebecca Shawcross (Shoe Collection, Northampton Borough Council); Ian Shields; Malcolm Shields; John Slater; Stephen Price; Sue Thacker; John Thorpe (*Yorkshire Post*); Bev Wickson and Jenni Williams.

Former employees of Benefit Footwear including William Clayton, Mrs E. Hunter, Mrs Johnson, Fred Lunn, Olive Smeatham, Robert Walker, Mrs A. M. Wilson and Mr W. H. Wiseman.

The following libraries and organisations that provided especially valuable assistance: Bristol Library; Cleveland County Libraries; Companies House; Coventry Central Library; Derby Local Studies Library; Hull Local History Library; Leeds Central Library; Leicester Central Library; Nottingham Central Library; Patent Office; Public Record Office; Sheffield Local Studies Library; Stockton-on-Tees Library; Suffolk Record Office; Surrey History Centre; Uttoxeter Heritage Centre; Wakefield Library; Warrington Central Library and Wilberforce House, Hull.

Illustration Acknowledgements

Every reasonable effort has been made to ascertain ownership of all illustrations used. Ownership or copyright of illustrations lies with the people and organisations listed. Information would be welcomed which would enable the rectification of any error.

The authors and publisher would like to thank the following people, museums, libraries and archives for permission to reproduce this material.

Anthony Bean, 66, 68, 71, 72, 74, 226; Birmingham Local Studies and History Centre, 75; Andrew Bolt, 49, 51; Bristol Library, 32; the late Bernard Brown, 22; Michael Brown, 236; P. & S. Butler, 156; Elsie Carl, 215 (photo: Keith Wade); City of Wakefield Library, 128; William Clayton, 216 (photo: Pickards of Wortley); Cleveland County Library, 124; Coventry Libraries and Information Services, 16; Cusworth Museum Hall Museum, Doncaster, 80; Derby City Libraries, 169; Derbyshire Library Service, Cultural and Community Services Department, 195; Doncaster Library and Information Services, 34, 79, 81; East Midlands Oral History Archive, 166; David Edwards, Flambards, 25, 227; Douglas R.P. Ferriday, 132; Paul Gibson Collection, 1, 29, 117, 130, 165; Andrew Gill Collection, front cover, 24; Goole Museum, East Riding of Yorkshire Museums and Galleries, 158; Arthur Hudson, 203, 205, 207, 208, 221; Hull Daily Mail Publications, 31, 200; Hull Local Studies Library, 26, 53, 65, 67, 73, 93, 141; Mrs E. Johnson, 172; Christopher Ketchell, Local History Unit, Hull College—from the collection of the late Dr Eric Sigsworth, 6, 7, 9, 89, 90; Leicestershire Library and Information Services, 112; Leodis Photographic Archive of Leeds, 206; Fred Lunn, 192; Tony Mackrill, 10, 230; Memory Lane Gallery, Hull, 97, 157; Newark and Sherwood Council and Nottingham County Council, 212; North Devon Athenaeum, 57, 58; Northamptonshire Libraries and Information Services, 160; Nottinghamshire County Council, 13; Daphne Palmer, 4, 5; People's Past and Present Archive, District of Easington Council, 198, 199; Stephen Price, 225; R.A. (Postcards) Ltd, London, 211; Saxone and Lilley & Skinner Group of Companies, 217-19; Ian and Malcolm Shields, 38, 40; Stockton-on-Tees Library, 42, 61, 62; Surrey History Service, 202; Uttoxeter Heritage Centre, 155, 210 (photo: Alfred McCann); Valentine & Sons Ltd, Dundee and London, 222, 224; Wilberforce House, Hull City Museums and Art Galleries, 187; W.H. Wiseman, 214; York Library, 85-7.

The following images, as well as those unnumbered in the book, are from private collections: 2, 3, 8, 11, 12, 14, 15, 17-21, 23, 27, 28, 30, 33, 35-7, 39, 41, 43-8, 50, 52, 54-6, 59, 60, 63, 64, 69, 70, 76, 77, 78, 82, 83, 84, 88, 91, 92, 94-6, 98-111, 113-15, 118-23, 125-7, 129, 131, 133-40, 142-53, 154, 159, 161-4, 167, 168, 170, 171, 173-86, 188-91, 193, 194, 196, 197, 201, 204, 209, 213, 228, 229, 231-5, 237, 238.

1 Good Prospects on Prospect Street

When William Franklin opened his first boot shop in Prospect Street, Hull, in 1875, Queen Victoria had been on the throne for 38 years and the telephone and phonograph had not yet been invented. Victorian England was the most prosperous country in the world—it was a time of great technological progress, enormous optimism and expansion.

The 26-year-old Franklin had grown up in an era characterised by rapid change, astonishing innovation and developments in nearly every sphere of life.

The population of Britain had increased by around two million people over the previous decade and this, combined with a new prosperity, fuelled the demand for all sorts of consumer goods. Like many of his fellow countrymen, the young Franklin would have had great confidence and optimism as he embarked on his first commercial enterprise in Hull. The success of his first small boot shop in Hull encouraged further expansion and from this modest beginning he developed a vast empire of boot stores that spread the length and breadth of the country.

William Franklin was born in the small village of Elton in Huntingdonshire in 1848, the eldest of 15 children of Richard and Eunice Franklin. Typical of 19th-century families, the Franklin family was large and patriarchal—encouraging hard work, social deference, respectability and religious conformity. The Franklins

1 *In 1875 the first Public Benefit Boot Company store was opened by William Henry Franklin at 93 Prospect Street, Hull. The business was further expanded into other premises on Prospect Street over the following years and by the turn of the century the street had developed into a busy retail area.*

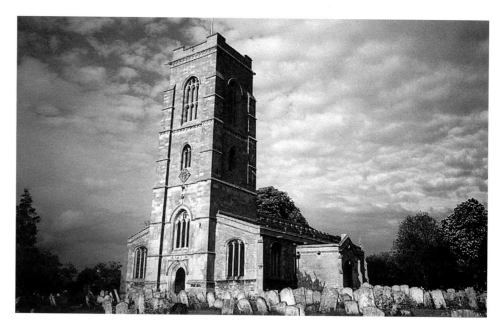

2 *The Parish Church at Elton, Huntingdonshire, where several generations of the Franklin family are buried. Amongst them are the grandparents of William and George Franklin as well as three of their brothers who died as infants.*

were bakers, grocers and drapers in the village. It is likely that William and his younger brothers gained valuable insight into the workings of the family businesses in their home village. They would have seen first-hand what was required to succeed—hard work, long hours, self-sacrifice and commitment. They would also be aware of the ups and downs experienced by family businesses.

William attended school in Elton and as the village had four shoemakers in the early 1860s, he may have been subsequently apprenticed to one of them. His father may have seen boot-making as an '*up and coming*' profession as at the time the footwear industry was experiencing rapid change. Great innovations in mechanisation were developed and some were adopted from North America to facilitate the production of cheap footwear. Mechanisation replaced many of the hand processes that had been performed in cottages for generations. The character of cities, towns and villages changed dramatically as numerous factories were erected to accommodate the workers and their rows of new machinery.

In the 1861 census of Elton, William who would have been aged 13 at the time, is not in the household with his family, so it is possible that he had already embarked on a shoemaking apprenticeship and was making his own way in the world.

The patriarch of the Franklin family, George Franklin died in 1825 at the age of seventy-seven. His headstone in the Elton churchyard tells of a man:

> ... of exemplary sobriety and honesty, of a refined and peaceful disposition, and was from early life thoughtful and salubrious. His mind was richly stored with

interesting knowledge of the beauties of Creation and Redemption and he was blessed through life with almost uninterrupted health which the gracious hand of Providence frequently entails on temperance.

After the death of William's grandfather John in 1865, Richard Franklin and his family of eight children moved from Elton to Grimsby on the east coast of Lincolnshire. Richard again operated a bakery and grocery business in Grimsby as he had done previously in Elton. His second son George also worked in the grocery business during this period.

3 The Franklin residence (centre of photograph) in the village of Elton where the Franklin family lived from around 1789.

Records indicate that William was involved in the boot trade in Leeds in the early 1870s, but in what capacity has not been established. Footwear centres such as Leicester, Leeds, Northampton and London, were by that time well established and expanding rapidly.

During the 1870s the town of Hull was spreading due to a growing population—largely brought about by many industries connected to the port, such as timber and oil seed crushing. New docks were constructed to accommodate the booming trades and the railways made possible far better trading links with other

4 The simplicity of the family drapery and grocery store in Elton gave little hint of the large manufacturing and retail empire that was subsequently built by the Franklins.

areas of the country. Hull was still called a town and it was not until 1897, the year of Queen Victoria's Diamond Jubilee, that Hull was proclaimed a city. At that time little wholesale footwear manufacture took place in the region, so it is likely that footwear was more expensive in Hull than in many other major centres.

William Franklin saw this as a good business opportunity and in 1875 opened a small shop at 93 Prospect Street, Hull, initially trading under the title of Public Benefit Boot and Shoe Company. The title, later shortened to The Public Benefit Boot Company, seems most unwieldy today, but the words *public* and *benefit* probably carried appropriate and lofty connotations, that were highly regarded in the Victorian era.

The first shop site was chosen carefully on a very busy thoroughfare, close to the town's general infirmary and within easy reach of the railway station. Stock would be transported by train from Bradford and Leeds, then picked up by cart and taken the short distance to Franklin's retail outlet. By bringing in his wares from Bradford and Leeds he could be assured of the keenest prices and the very best quality.

The shop at 93 Prospect Street was probably a very basic facility, as were most of the early boot retail outlets. Many were dimly lit with oil lamps and there was often no comfortable seating, no mirrors nor carpets to cover the bare floorboards. Boots were hung outside on pegs with price tags attached and in this way potential customers could feel and view the merchandise without venturing inside the shop. The crowded shop window would display masses of boots and shoes. Scores of boots hung from the shop ceiling and the strong smell of leather would have permeated the interior of the store. Often the owner lived above the shop for added security and working hours would be very long, especially on a Saturday when in the evening most workers were paid. A *cash only* basis was the recognised way of trading.

5 *The Franklin residence at Elton, photographed late in the 19th century. Ladies relax in the garden at the rear of the property.*

Immediate success in Hull meant a speedy expansion into premises at numbers 16 and 92 Prospect Street. William Franklin, like some of his competitors, began seeking partnerships to expand his business further—he had commenced the exciting journey of building an enterprise that was to become one of the world's major multiple footwear retailers.

As the pace quickened it was soon apparent that, although a brilliant start had been made with his enterprise, there were obstacles to be overcome. His

6 The closing and preparation room in a late 19th-century boot factory. The largely immigrant workforce performed the more menial tasks. The only form of lighting in this factory was daylight. There is no evidence of gas or steam piping so it is assumed that the machines were pedal-powered. Punches are displayed on the bench – indicating hand operation rather than the use of machines. The appearance of many young girls in the photograph suggests cheap labour. There were a lot of different processes being conducted in this room where heavy working boots were being manufactured.

business began on a basis of factoring—that is, buying in manufactured footwear rather than self-manufacturing. Franklin could see that other successful operators in the boot trade had their own manufacturing capability. Without his own manufacturing plant he felt he had little say in the actual style, quality and price of his wares and he was aware that it was common for some manufacturers to go out of business quickly. Supplies could be *ad hoc* and Franklin would have to search for another supplier of the same quality and price he demanded for his stores.

7 An early shoe factory, possibly in the Leeds area. The powerhouse with a huge bell tower suggests that the factory was steam-powered.

Another problem was the matter of repairs associated with the sale of foot-wear, especially considering the large turnover he was achieving. To solve this he opened a small repair facility at 88–89 West Parade, Hull. The premises were located within easy reach of his shops and Franklin employed a shoemaker named James Eccles to repair the boots and shoes.

The next important step was to find a good, reliable supplier of quality footwear. In Leeds Franklin came across hand-made boot samples produced by three brothers—George, Brow and John Dickinson. The Dickinson brothers had commenced manufacturing footwear in a tiny room in their parents' house at Bramley near Leeds.

8 The Briton trademark that was used from 1874 by Dickinson Brothers of Bramley near Leeds. The trademark was eventually registered on 20 September 1887. Many years later the Briton Boot was still claimed to be 'the best and cheapest Working Man's boot in England'.

9 Bottoming Department in a footwear factory of the 1890s where there is evidence of numerous belt-driven overhead drive machines. The machine in the foreground is a sole leveller.

With a keen eye for an opportunity he saw huge potential in the boots produced from this fledgling enterprise. The Dickinsons had low overheads and were doubtless anxious to please; to this end, they kept their prices reasonable and the quality high. Franklin offered the brothers contracts to supply footwear to the Public Benefit Boot and Shoe Company. This in turn greatly encouraged the brothers and they began manufacturing in earnest throughout the 1870s. They worked steadily towards the 1880 opening of their factory in Bramley at which time they employed 60 workers. So was born a legend—the famous *Benefit* boot. A decade later Dickinson Brothers had 160 employees and produced 5,000 pairs of boots per week from the factory they built in Swinnow Road, Leeds. One of the brothers, Brow Dickinson, went on to become the highly respected managing director of the Public Benefit Boot Company and a prominent member of the Leeds community.

2 Great will be the Coming of this Boot Company

From the outset, William Franklin involved various members of his family in helping to build his dream. He needed reliable hard-working people who would not demand high wages and a number of family members rallied to the cause. Most prominent amongst them was William's younger brother George. He had married Elizabeth Hunn in Grimsby in 1872 and by 1874 he had moved to Hull where he worked for a short period in his father's Trinity Street grocery store.

By 1880 the two brothers William and George were leasing a series of boot shops side by side in London Road, Derby. At first they traded under the name of Franklin Brothers but, soon after, the business took on the same Public Benefit title as the Hull store. Trade directory entries show that this initial leasing of stores under the name of Franklin Brothers was a common practice in other parts

10 *William Henry Franklin, 1848-1907, founder of the Public Benefit Boot Company.*

of the country. They were possibly testing the water before making further business commitments. In the 1881 census, the two Franklin brothers are listed as boot manufacturers, not boot-retailers, which suggests by this time they had made a definite commitment to manufacturing their own footwear—probably involving some formal arrangement with Brow Dickinson and another manufacturer in Leicester.

Perhaps the greatest behind-the-scenes contribution was that made by Richard, father of William and George. He was listed in the 1881 census as aged 55, with his occupation given merely as an assistant in a boot shop. His previous lifelong family business experiences would have been priceless, offering his services in a practical way. This allowed William greater freedom to move around his various trading regions, safe in the knowledge that his Hull shops were in reliable hands. Richard Franklin provided some initial financial backing for the purchase of premises in Hull and elsewhere. His role of adviser would have been invaluable and no doubt he was a central rallying figure, as a father often is, to gather support from the rest of the family.

Other siblings of William and George—Louisa aged 18 and Fred aged 15—were also listed in the 1881 census as assistants in a boot shop, as was Jonathan Rose, a lodger in the Franklin household at the time. Jonathan Rose in due course went on to become a company shareholder and to manage a major Public Benefit branch in Wakefield.

From the 1880s a major series of store openings took place as new branches opened in Bristol, Coventry, Stockton-on-Tees, Derby, Nottingham and Beverley.

11 Public Benefit opened a branch at 102 Fishergate, Preston, around the time in 1903 that this photograph was taken. The premises were located in the building on the left with the large canopy. In the distance can be seen the Town Hall with its clock tower – the building was later destroyed by fire and demolished. The other building with a tower belonged to the Preston Gas Company and has since been demolished.

12 By 1910 the company had established another branch at 168 Friargate, Preston. In this view looking down Friargate, the premises were situated on the right-hand side of Friargate at the junction of Orchard Street.

In every case, the prominent sites were carefully chosen and the overseer of the branch would be a trusted friend or member of the extended family. These people became area managers responsible for promoting further business from these newly opened branches and they went about this task with obvious pride and the promise of greater rewards.

As the Public Benefit business grew, it needed to be self-funding at all times to succeed. Often, an existing footwear shop in the right location would be refitted to trade under the common Public Benefit name. The previous manager was often retained and sometimes became a shareholder.

Public Benefit worked on the principle of selling footwear at wholesale prices that made their wares cheaper and allowed them to sell large quantities—achieving a regular turnover and a quick profit. That profit was constantly ploughed back into the business, enabling new stores to be opened in even more strategic locations.

George Franklin's uncle, Jabez Harker (trading as J. Harker and Company), had successfully developed the business in the prominent Albert Hall Buildings in Nottingham. This grand emporium was established by 1881 and was

13 In Nottingham from 1881 the company occupied the grand Albert Hall Buildings, named after the nearby Albert Hall concert hall. The right side of the company premises are still standing – the other half has been demolished and replaced with a building that retains many of the design features of the original building.

14 The wooden structure of Albert Hall, adjacent to the Public Benefit premises in Nottingham, caught fire on 22 April 1906. This postcard depicting the event was posted two days later.

15 *The company presence in Derby began in 1880 when they occupied premises at 24-28 London Street between Traffic Street and St Peter's Street up until 1895. The former Congregational Chapel can be seen on the right and the company premises were located on the left a little past the Raleigh Cycles sign. On her visit to Derby on 21 May 1891, Queen Victoria travelled down London Road to the nearby Infirmary but there is no record of whether she stopped at The Public Benefit Boot Company store to be fitted with a pair of black shoes.*

16 *In the early 1880s Samuel Harker commenced trading on Smithford Street, Coventry, initially under his own name, then by the mid-1880s under the title 'The Great Boot Hall'. By the early 1900s the premises also traded under the title 'The Public Benefit Boot Company', seen here on the canopy.*

17 *Engraved button hook used to make life easier in the days of button-up boots. The hook was possibly given away as a promotional item with the purchase of button-up boots.*

a forerunner of many other outstanding premises that were soon to be seen throughout the towns and cities of England. Jabez Harker heavily promoted trade both in Nottingham and the surrounding district and over the next few years he worked energetically to expand the business with his nephews William and George Franklin.

Jabez Harker's older brother Samuel was also deeply involved with the Public Benefit Boot Company. He was a successful lace manufacturer but by the early 1880s he had become a boot dealer trading at 40-41 Smithford Street, Coventry. He initially traded at this address as 'The Great Boot Hall' operated by S. Harker & Company but by the early 1900s the premises also carried the title 'Public Benefit Boot Company' under the management of S. Harker & Son. Samuel Harker's four children were used in various ways in the business; his son Frederick continued to manage the Coventry business for many years after his father's death in 1907, and Samuel Harker's brother-in-law Samuel Burton managed the Public Benefit store at Rugby.

Jabez Harker's children were also associated with the business over many years. His daughter Elizabeth assisted in the Peterborough store; his son-in-law John Taylor managed the Public Benefit branch at Luton; and Jabez's son William managed at various times the Public Benefit branches at Peterborough, Chester and Bolton.

The involvement in the business over many decades of more than twenty members of the Franklin and Harker families must have been a significant stabilising factor in the company's growth and success. Over the years Franklin and Harker siblings, uncles, cousins and in-laws managed Public Benefit branches in counties as widespread as Bedfordshire, Cambridgeshire, Cheshire, Derbyshire, Lancashire, Lincolnshire, Nottinghamshire, Warwickshire and Yorkshire.

In the early years of the business, boot and shoe repairs were undertaken efficiently at various centres. In Hull repairs were made at the considerably

18 *A branch was opened at 20 Upper Union Street in the busy Devon town of Torquay around 1890. This branch was one of many owned and controlled by Lennards of Bristol and around 1914 the Public Benefit trading name was replaced with the Lennards' name. By 1929 the company was also operating another branch at 45 Union Street, Torquay.*

19 *The Public Benefit premises can be seen on the right in this 1920s postcard of High Row in the prosperous town of Darlington, 11 miles from the Stockton branch. In 1896 the company had a store at 19 High Row, Darlington, and around 1910 they moved to 43 High Row.*

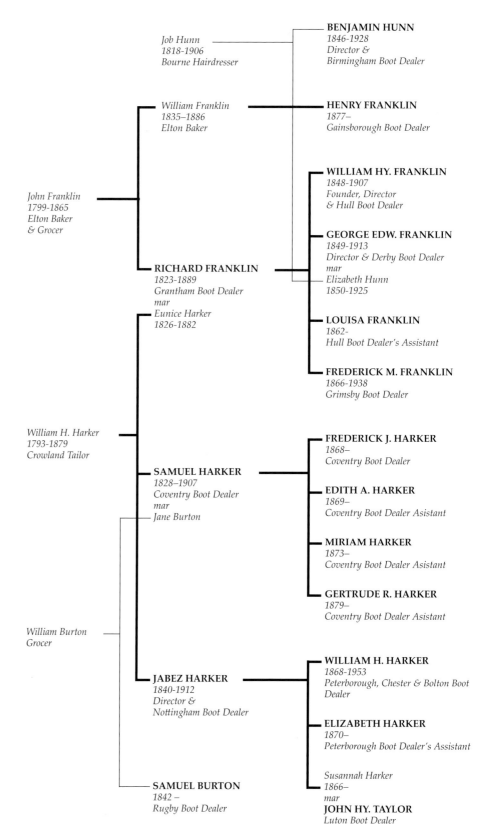

*20 Benjamin Hunn 1846-1928
(above left), brother-in-law of
George Franklin, managed the
Public Benefit Boot Company
stores in the Birmingham area.*

*21 Jabez Harker 1840-1912
(above right), uncle of William
and George Franklin, managed
the company's operations in the
Nottingham region.*

*Right: Simplified chart showing
the relationship between some of
the Franklin and Harker family
members who were directly associated with the Public Benefit Boot
Company. Individuals whose name
appears in bold capital letters had
a direct involvement with the
company, some of them for thirty
years or more.*

*Job Hunn
1818-1906
Bourne Hairdresser*

BENJAMIN HUNN
*1846-1928
Director &
Birmingham Boot Dealer*

*William Franklin
1835–1886
Elton Baker*

HENRY FRANKLIN
*1877–
Gainsborough Boot Dealer*

*John Franklin
1799-1865
Elton Baker
& Grocer*

WILLIAM HY. FRANKLIN
*1848-1907
Founder, Director
& Hull Boot Dealer*

GEORGE EDW. FRANKLIN
*1849-1913
Director & Derby Boot Dealer
mar
Elizabeth Hunn
1850-1925*

RICHARD FRANKLIN
*1823-1889
Grantham Boot Dealer
mar
Eunice Harker
1826-1882*

LOUISA FRANKLIN
*1862-
Hull Boot Dealer's Assistant*

FREDERICK M. FRANKLIN
*1866-1938
Grimsby Boot Dealer*

*William H. Harker
1793-1879
Crowland Tailor*

FREDERICK J. HARKER
*1868–
Coventry Boot Dealer*

EDITH A. HARKER
*1869–
Coventry Boot Dealer Asistant*

SAMUEL HARKER
*1828–1907
Coventry Boot Dealer
mar
Jane Burton*

MIRIAM HARKER
*1873–
Coventry Boot Dealer Asistant*

GERTRUDE R. HARKER
*1879–
Coventry Boot Dealer Asistant*

*William Burton
Grocer*

WILLIAM H. HARKER
*1868-1953
Peterborough, Chester & Bolton Boot
Dealer*

JABEZ HARKER
*1840-1912
Director &
Nottingham Boot Dealer*

ELIZABETH HARKER
*1870–
Peterborough Boot Dealer's Assistant*

*Susannah Harker
1866–
mar*
JOHN HY. TAYLOR
Luton Boot Dealer

SAMUEL BURTON
*1842 –
Rugby Boot Dealer*

expanded premises at 90–94 Prospect Street. Repairs were also performed at the purpose-built Nottingham facility and the spacious Derby premises at 24–28 London Road. The Stockton and Bristol premises were large enough to carry out repairs from those towns and surrounding areas—as well as carry stock for distribution purposes.

Newspaper advertisements and trade directory entries published in 1882 show how William Franklin held a strong presence in Hull, Leicester and London. Further rapid expansion took place into Lincolnshire, with various Franklin family members managing the stores in Gainsborough and Grimsby. Text in the early company advertisements proclaimed 'fresh supplies from our factories daily', giving the impression of a large organisation, although the company was less than a decade old. It is highly likely that 'our factories' actually referred to the Dickinson factory at Bramley and a factory in Leicester operating under the name Lennard Brothers.

As Franklin opened stores in Leicester, Bath, London and Bristol he would have undoubtedly needed a good local supplier of stock and there was no supplier better placed than Lennard Brothers in Leicester. The relationship that developed between the Franklins and Lennards eventually became an integral part of the Public Benefit story.

22 *George Edward Franklin, 1849-1913, whose company responsibilities centred around the Derby region.*

Brow Dickinson was encouraged to expand the retail outlets into the North East, using Stockton as a base and by adding stores in Hartlepool, West Hartlepool, Middlesbrough, Thornaby, Redcar and eventually Coatham. Thus the idea was born of dividing the country into territories and placing a trusted man at the helm to promote further expansion in each region.

In 1883 and 1884 stores were opened in Stockport and Stafford as well as Hanley, and Belper in the Derby region. Ilkeston followed under an alliance formed between George Franklin and Jabez Harker. William Franklin continued his mission to find suitable business partners and sought out John Kirby—an old

23 *The Public Benefit Boot Company trademark that was registered 27 February 1883.*

acquaintance known to him and Brow Dickinson. John Kirby, an accomplished bootmaker, had considerable business interests in Chesterfield and Sheffield and his brother George Kirby, also a bootmaker, had similar interests in Warrington and Widnes.

George Franklin also developed business links with his brother-in-law Benjamin Hunn. He was originally a chemist and druggist, but in the early 1880s he too joined his in-laws in the Public Benefit Boot and Shoe Company and spearheaded development in the Birmingham region. Jabez Harker and George Franklin opened the Loughborough premises in 1885. In the space of a decade a vast network of enterprises had been forged from Stockton in the North East through the industrialised Midlands to Bristol in the west. The network consisted of strong partnerships ensuring reliable supply along with efficient distribution and repair capabilities.

Throughout the 1880s and 1890s and possibly over a longer period, one of the most colourful forms of the Public Benefit Boot and Shoe Company's advertising blitz was a giant-size boot that was regularly paraded around Yorkshire towns and villages on a flat horse-drawn cart. The rim of the boot was about four metres above the road and the drivers figure emerged from the top of the boot. A man ringing a bell and calling out the numerous virtues of Benefit Boots usually preceded the enormous horse-drawn boot.

In Bristol, Henry Lennard registered the horse-drawn boot as a trademark in 1883 although it may have been in use as an advertising gimmick for some time prior to that. It certainly became a well-known and fondly remembered symbol of the company. It is probable that there were a number of these giant horse-drawn boots in various parts of the country as the trademark was used as far afield as Bristol, Birmingham, Hull and Nottingham. The unique trademark was applied to a multitude of company promotional and advertising material and appeared on the store's glass lampshades, signs, labels and on various items that were given to customers such as button hooks and shoehorns.

In 1885 a decision to upgrade selected locations was made and the premises in Hull were the first to be transformed. Continued expansion called for a large purpose-built store designed to appeal to men and women of all ages. The new Hull premises on Prospect Street replaced the four smaller stores occupied over the previous decade. This very impressive building was the first in a series to be purpose-built across the nation over the next few years. In exactly the same way

24 *The large boot on the dray was pulled around from village to village to remind people that the company had a presence in the vicinity.*

25 *The trademark was used prominently on much of the company's advertising and promotional material. The large horse-drawn boot was often featured in store illustrations and on numerous other items such as shoehorns, posters, signs, etc.*

26 One of the early Public Benefit
Boot Company advertisements
that flagged the opening of their
Prospect Street premises on 2 May
1885. 'Look out! Look out! for the
grand opening day of the Public
Benefit Boot Company's large
mammoth premises opposite the
infirmary, Hull.' The company
was also signalling a huge
expansion programme.

'It may interest many to know
that these are the first of a series
of similar buildings which they
are about to erect at Nottingham,
Derby, Bristol, Birmingham and
Sheffield and other large towns
to meet the extension of their
businesses in these places.'

LOOK OUT!   LOOK OUT!!
GRAND   OPENING   FOR THE
                    DAY
PUBLIC   BENEFIT   BOOT   COMPANY'S
                    OF THE

LARGE MAMMOTH PREMISES,
Opposite the infirmary, HULL,
Corner of ALBION-STREET, PROSPECT-STREET,
On SATURDAY, May 2nd.
The Largest Boot and Shoe Establishment
in the World.
With the Largest Stocks of
Ladies', Gentlemen's, Boy's and Girls' BOOTS and
SHOES in Yorkshire.
Working Men's and Boys' NAILED BOOTS,
At astounding Low Prices.
LAWN TENNIS, CRICKET, and SAND SHOES,
Cheapest in Hull.

Come and see our Windows and Judge for
yourselves.

Don't forget the Grand Opening Day,
SATURDAY, MAY 2ND,
At our Mammoth Premises,
Corner of
ALBION-STREET, PROSPECT-STREET
(Just opposite the Infirmary),
HULL.

It may interest many to know that
these are the first of a series of similar
buildings which they are about to erect at
Nottingham, Derby, Bristol, Birmingham,
and Sheffield, and other large Towns, to meet
the extension of their Businesses in these
places.

27 For at least 70 years the
company traded on busy Bridge
Street in Warrington. This branch
would have supplied boots to
the regoin's chemical industry
workforce as well as workers
involved in the local brewing,
soap-making, wire-making, iron
and steel, textiles, engineering,
tanning and allied industries.

28 No.78 Lichfield Road,
Birmingham, shown here 1900-10,
was clearly a well-established
branch by this time. On a corner
site, the manageress and her
three asistants pose for this
company photograph. The window
displays are stacked high, but
are unlikely to have real variety.
This important branch was one of
around half a dozen operated by
the company in this region.

29 *The premises of the Public Benefit Boot Company in Prospect Street, Hull, in the early part of the century. The building was originally a Temperance Hotel before it was converted into the prestigious company headquarters in the Hull region. The company occupied this building from May 1885 until May 1941.*

that the manufacturing processes had transformed the boot trade, it was now time for the retailing side of the business to undergo major change. Rather than the former frugal no-frills premises, the customers were now invited to purchase their footwear in large elegant emporiums.

An article published in the *Hull News* on 2 May 1885 proudly describes the new building as a 'fine, handsome and substantial erection':

> The new premises at the corner of Prospect Street and Albion Street built by the Public Benefit Boot & Shoe Co will be opened for business today (Saturday), built to suit the requirements of the Company's very large business. The New building, although not strictly speaking of an ornate or classic style of architecture, is a fine handsome and substantial erection, and will add one to the number of new structures which have done not a little to improve the third port in recent years. The height of the building from the basement to the tips of the turrets is 80 feet, whilst the ground area is no less than 1800 feet the width of frontage 111 feet. On the bottom floor to the front are the Ladies Saloon, Gentlemen's Saloon, General Sales room, stock and show shop, and what may be termed a 'Coach and four' goods entrance. It is a four storey red stock brick building with grey stone facings elaborately

carved and granite base, the whole being surmounted by two slate turrets and railings tipped with gold, as are the massive window frames.

The article went on to describe how a nine-foot-wide staircase made of pitch pine reached up to each floor. The walls and floors were also made of polished pitch pine except for the Ladies' Saloon, which was treated in fine old English oak. In this department the ladies had cushioned seats and exquisitely carved screens with stained glass depicting birds and human figures. A retiring room was made available for ladies after transacting their business. Finally the rather long article goes on to say 'there are enough boots and shoes in the new premises to supply the whole of Hull and the East Riding'.

A company advertisement on the same page of the 2 May 1885 edition of the *Hull News* claimed the 'mammoth premises' to be 'the largest boot and shoe establishment in the world'. By using extensive advertising campaigns, as in the case of this large branch opening in Hull, the company ensured the success of its considerable investment.

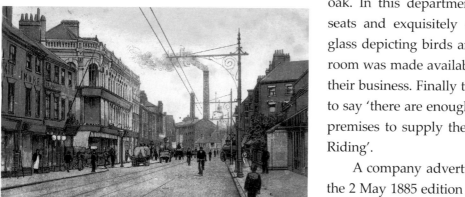

30 Smoke billows from the chimneys of Blundell's Mill that formed a backdrop to Prospect Street in Hull, a reminder of that city's industrial heritage.

31 This busy turn-of-the-century scene shows the Hull branch on the corner of Prospect Street and Albion Street with a city tram passing by. The view looks towards Beverley Road with Blundell's Mill in the distance. Blundell's Mill has disappeared and The Hull Daily Mail buildings are now in that vicinity.

With the stage set, trusted partnerships in place and territories established, the next phase of rapid promotion of the brand name began in earnest. By now the company was developing a solid reputation for sound business sense and imitators were trying to capitalise on the company name. So much so that George Franklin was prompted to place an advertisement in the *Loughborough Herald* denouncing such imitators and practices when the Loughborough branch was opened in 1885:

> CAUTION! CAUTION!! CAUTION!!! We caution the public against SMALL Dealers calling themselves the Public Benefit Boot Company. We have only One Establishment in Loughborough, exactly Opposite Sharrard's and Next Door to Claypole's and have no connection whatever with SMALL DEALERS and MARKET STALLMEN.
>
> Our Establishments are HULL, SHEFFIELD, BRISTOL, DERBY, NOTTINGHAM, COVENTRY, RIPLEY, BELPER, ILKESTON, WAKEFIELD, LOUGHBOROUGH, & c. The Company are the Largest Boot Manufacturers in Great Britain, their Goods are made to Wear, and every pair is sold at Wholesale Prices. Be sure and come direct to the Shop, and mind the Address.
>
> THE ORIGINAL PUBLIC BENEFIT BOOT CO., No 6, CHURCH–GATE, LOUGHBOROUGH Opposite SHARRARD'S, Next Door to CLAYPOLE'S And No Connection with others in the same street.

The Public Benefit Boot & Shoe Co., 38, High Street.—This company during the ten years they have been established have built up a widespread trade and reputation. From the very commencement of the business it was plainly evident, that if well-directed enterprise, liberal and honourable methods, could accomplish anything, this house would become the leading one. That it has become so is admitted on all sides, and moreover its connections and popularity are still greatly increasing, a result as gratifying as it is well deserved. The premises in occupation are four-storied, possessing a very attractive appearance, and comprising a spacious, handsomely fitted shop with a well-arranged show window, and very commodious warehouse. The stock is a very extensive one, including gents', ladies', boys', and children's boots and shoes, of all sorts, sizes, and fittings. A speciality is also made of boots and shoes particularly adapted to the industrial classes, and it is in this branch that the company have prospered beyond their most sanguine anticipations. Their goods are characterised throughout by sound workmanship, excellent design and finish, and thorough efficiency, the system of business being to supply these at the lowest possible prices consistent with quality, depending on the extent of the trade done for a proper remuneration. The management of this establishment is in thoroughly competent hands, prompt and polite attention being always secured. Persons wishing good value for their money will find there is no better house in Bristol.

32 Company details as they appeared in 'Bristol: An alphabetically arranged guide to the industrial resources of the ancient Royal and free city – leading merchants and manufacturers of Bristol and Bath, 1888'.

Following the huge success of the new branch in Prospect Street, Hull, the Smithford Street premises in Coventry received a similar upgrade. The Wakefield premises at 105 Kirkgate were opened in October 1885 with Jonathan Rose in charge. A handbill distributed in Wakefield at the time proclaimed:

GREAT WILL BE THE COMING OF THIS BOOT COMPANY!

They are coming in their TRUE NAME 'The Public Benefit' the title adopted and registered ten years ago

They are coming in their WELL-EARNED national renown, and their well-deserved world-wide fame!

They are coming in their REAL CHARACTER the largest cash retail and whole-sale dealers in Great Britain!

They are coming in their POSITIVE POWER the best value producers at the charges in England or the world!

They are coming in their GREAT STRENGTH the heaviest stock providers of every British and foreign variety!

They are coming in their FULL MIGHT the reducers of dishonest prices and destroyers of inferior qualities!

They are coming in their STRONG FORCE the rulers of the trade and presidents of the boot and shoe business!

They are coming in their REPUTATION the givers of all good and perfect boots and savers of the people's money!

Premises in Derby and other towns expanded in the same way—as the adjoining properties became available they would be snapped up by the company and used to extend the business. As the 1880s closed further significant upgrades of premises took place at the Moorhead in Sheffield and at 42 Corporation Street, Birmingham.

The extensive range of merchandise available during this period can be gauged from the following column of 21 Public Benefit classified advertisements appearing in a Hull newspaper in May 1889. The advertisements describe items available from the Prospect Street branch in Hull:

> Girls' Fancy Straps, strong sides, sizes 7–10, 1s 11d.
> Girls' strong Button Boots, 1s 11d–3s 11d.
> Boys' Goloshed Balmorals, Leyant legs, peak caps, sizes 11–13, 3s 4d, sizes 2–5, 3s 11d.
> Our noted strong Lace Boots for boys, 2s 6d, 3s 6d, 4s 6d—unequalled for hard work.
> Men's strong Lace Boots, straight toe caps, studded bottoms, 3s 11d.
> Kid leather-lined Lace Boots, 3s 11d—working men ask to see them.
> Men's Goloshed Balmorals, straight toe caps, all sizes, sewn, a wonder, 4s 11d.
> M. K. Kid Leather-lined Lace Boots and Leather-lined Button Boots, 3s 11d.
> See our enormous variety in Ladies Walking Shoes, sewn, 2s 11d, 3s 11d, and 4s 11d, selling in larger quantities than ever.
> Our Ladies Morocco Oxford Shoes—the talk of the Trade.

33 The Public Benefit Boot Company had a presence in Scarborough from 1909 until 1968. Early in the century they occupied these premises at 9 Westborough.

34 *In this 1890s Doncaster scene, the imposing building on the right is the Public Benefit Boot Company premises at 41-45 St Sepulchre Street. Boots were displayed in the front window and a sign in a second-floor window advertised 'Boys' & Girls' School Boots'. The company occupied these premises from the very early 1890s until their new building was completed next door in 1898.*

35 *The company premises on the corner of St Sepulchre Street and Printing Office Street, Doncaster, in 1904. The building they occupied previously can be easily distinguished next door.*

Girls' Kid Oxford Shoes, fancy vamps, sizes 7, 8, 9, and 10s, 2s 9d; sizes 11, 12, 13 and 14, 3s 9d; selling as fast as we can make them.
Children's High-leg Kid Button Boots, 2s 11d.
Fancy Patent Vamps 3s 11d—ask to see them—the talk of the trade.

36 Sheffield remained a major centre throughout the history of the company and they occupied premises on this prominent Moorhead intersection for more than 60 years. From her high pedestal Queen Victoria watches over the activity. The scene was a popular subject for postcards over the years.

Children's Fancy-strap Shoes—the newest goods out, in kid, morocco, and seal—enormous demand for these goods.

Mothers ask to see our latest style in Children's Button Boots, fancy patent vamps and kid scolloped tops, sizes 2–5, 1s 11d—the talk of the trade.

Men's Cloth-top Oxford Shoes, 4s 11d, Calf-sewn Oxford Shoes, 5s 11d—with out an equal in the trade.

Men's Oxford Shoes—ask to see them.

Men's French Calf Bals, red in top, 6s 11d, calf lined through, 7s 11d—selling in enormous quantities.

Girls' strong Laced Boots, red top, studded soles, made expressly for school children—cannot be equaled for hard wear—sizes 7 to 10, 2s 6d—other qualities much cheaper.

The Briton 'Boot,' a real hide upper bellowed, best English sole, hand-wrought studs, wide fitting, all sizes, 7s 11d, the best and cheapest Working Man's boot in England.

Ladies High-lag Cloth Lace Boots, sewn, 6s 11d, Ladies High-leg Kid Button Boots, fancy scollop vamp, 5s 11d—selling year after year. Ladies Kid Blocks, 4s 7 1/2d, Ladies Fancy Patent Cap, 4s 11d, superior qualities, sewn, 5s 11d.

For all the latest style in boots and shoes. Large deliveries every week direct from our own factories. See our windows—Prospect Street, Hull.

The myriad of different footwear styles suggests that good sources of supply were available to the Public Benefit proprietors. Many of their main competitors began by manufacturing footwear and subsequently expanded into retailing. Franklin did not essentially own any factories—they belonged to the Dickinsons and the Lennards and each manufacturer produced very distinct footwear styles. Franklin's stock was easily transportable by rail and would undoubtedly be available in all of the Public Benefit shops. Some of their competitors would have struggled to stock the same diversity of footwear.

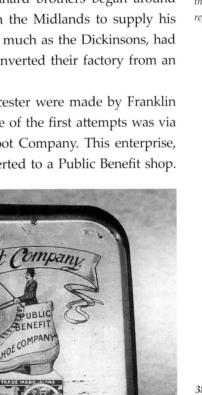

37 The Public Benefit Boot Company premises at The Moorhead, Sheffield, depicted around 1920. By very early in the 1900s trams were running regularly past The Moorhead store.

William Franklin's relationship with the Lennard brothers began around 1880 with the need for a good supplier based in the Midlands to supply his latest retail ventures in the region. The Lennards, much as the Dickinsons, had begun manufacturing boots and shoes, having converted their factory from an established hosiery manufacture to footwear.

Early attempts to establish a presence in Leicester were made by Franklin around 1882 in the heart of Lennard territory. One of the first attempts was via an established business trading as The Cheap Boot Company. This enterprise, managed by Rupert Ball, was subsequently converted to a Public Benefit shop.

38 The company was using unique forms of advertising from the early 1880s. Their memorable trademark was featured inside the lid of a tin given to customers as a Christmas promotion in the 1890s.

*39 A branch of The Mutual
Stores, of which only a handful
ever came into being, is evident
on the left (opposite the clock) in
this mid-1890s image of High
Street, Winchester. This trading
name was registered specifically
to challenge a major rival – in
this case, Freeman, Hardy and
Willis. A few years later the
threat diminished and by 1897 the
branch was trading as The Public
Benefit Boot Company.*

*40 Tin produced in the 1890s by
the company depicts the Bristol
headquarters of Lennards Limited
and lists their numerous branches.*

This arrangement lasted about two years and was abandoned for another formal
agreement in 1884 to trade in Belgrave Gate, Leicester. Managed by John Green,
the Belgrave Gate premises were extended at that time.

Franklin had also established a store in High Street, Bristol, in 1880. By 1883
Henry Lennard, a boot factor and one of the Lennard brothers, was managing

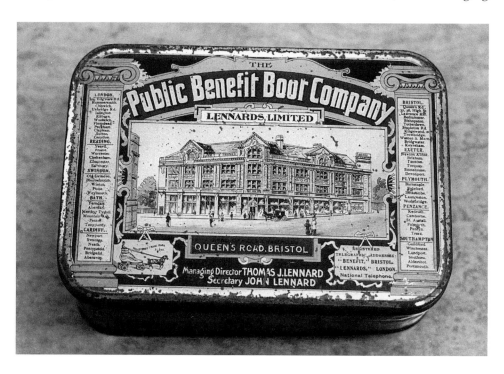

the Bristol store trading as the Public Benefit Boot and Shoe Company.

An agreement was also reached for the Leicester branch to be managed by Lennard Brothers. The Leicester-based brothers' involvement was initially in the management of premises opened by Franklin and in supplying him with stock. This was typical of Franklin's style of management—to establish a presence in a region and then to seek either an arrangement or a partnership agreement that would leave him free to develop the business in other areas.

Throughout the late 1880s Lennard Brothers, under the leadership of Samuel Lennard, opened further outlets in Bristol and Leicester and continued to trade under the Public Benefit name.

By the early 1890s Samuel Lennard was casting his eyes further afield and he opened stores in Portsmouth, Bournemouth and Winton in 1894, and two shops in Plymouth in 1895. Due to strong competition from a major rival, these stores opened rapidly under a mix of trading titles—Lennard Brothers and Mutual Boot Stores and not as the Public Benefit Boot Company. In this same period 1890-95, Franklin had been also opening more shops—in Wales, Bath, Redruth, Truro, Swindon, and Torquay and in many areas of London.

In 1896 Samuel Lennard's younger and well-educated brother Thomas forged agreement with the Franklin board to expand quickly the use of the single company name of Public Benefit Boot Company right across his stores. Thomas Lennard could see the success of the arrangement his brother Samuel had with Franklin to operate eight Public Benefit Boot Company branches in Bristol and two branches in Leicester.

Further agreements, even down to full partnerships, would be most advantageous but Samuel had apparently not capitalised on any of these

41 Public Benefit opened a branch at 36 High Street in Stratford-on-Avon around 1908 and by 1913 they were trading there under the Lennards' name. In the 1920s there were two branches – the one on High Street and another at 30 Wood Street. The company premises cannot be seen on this historic section of High Street where the 16th-century Harvard House, the Town Hall and the Guild Chapel were located.

42 An announcement that appeared in the South Durham & Cleveland Mercury *and* Richmond Review *on 2 March 1894 for the opening of the West Hartlepool branch.*

ANOTHER TRIUMPH!

MAGNIFICENT OPENING

AT

WEST HARTLEPOOL.

THE PUBLIC BENEFIT BOOT CO., LTD.,

ARE THE ONLY

MANUFACTURING RETAILERS

IN THIS DISTRICT, AND CAN GIVE BETTER VALUE THAN ANY HOUSE IN THE TRADE. TRUE TO OUR NAME, WE

BENEFIT THE PUBLIC

DIRECT FROM FACTORY TO PEOPLE

IS OUR MOTTO.

Corner Lynn-street and Musgrave-street, WEST HARTLEPOOL
144, High-street, STOCKTON.
44, Linthorpe-road, MIDDLESBROUGH.

opportunities. Consequently Thomas Lennard set about founding a separate company to his brother's Lennard Brothers business. Thomas Lennard had prior links and partnerships with similar minded businessmen, just as Franklin had established earlier. In November 1896, in bringing those partnerships together Thomas Lennard made provision to buy all of the retail outlets from his brother Samuel Lennard. All of the three trading titles were purchased and Thomas

43 This prestigious branch was sited on the corner of Clock Tower and Cheapside, Leicester – from a postcard dated 24 February 1909. Leicester was an important branch for the company in the early days. The city was also the headquarters for many suppliers as well as Lennnard Brothers who were important allies.

44 Welford Place in Leicester where the Public Benefit Boot Company had manufacturing works from 1896 until at least 1911.

45 *The Grantham premises were situated for a decade on the extreme left of this view of London Road. Richard Franklin managed this branch and died on the premises in May 1889. Shortly after, the company moved to Market Place, Grantham, where they traded for another 65 years.*

46 *(below left) One of the many company premises in the London region was a branch at 3 Lavender Hill, Clapham. Opened in 1902, the store traded at this location for at least three decades. This turn-of-the-century scene captures the busy atmosphere of Lavender Hill at the time.*

began to manage the retailing venture more closely. Thus was born Lennards Limited.

Samuel Lennard continued as chairman of the Leicester-based Lennard Brothers manufacturing interests and remained a leading figure in the boot trade until his death in 1901.

47 *Public Benefit had a branch on High Road, Kilburn, in London's north-west from early in the 1900s. In 1916 they commenced trading under the Lennards' name and continued in that location until at least the 1930s.*

48 *(top) For more than 50 years the Public Benefit Boot Company traded in the Boston Market Place under the shadow of the 'Boston Stump'. The premises were located in the white corner building in the centre of this view, adjacent to a public house called the* Stump and Candle.

49 *(middle left) Ivegate, Bradford, where a company branch operated for many years. Early in the development of the business, William Franklin recognised the value of moving into the town of Bradford – close to the West Riding woollen industry with its towering mills and good rail links. He knew Bradford and Leeds well as places to obtain his supplies and sell them on at wholesale prices to the army of mill workers, railway workers and the general labouring classes.*

50 *(above) The grand Sunbridge Road area of Bradford was where Public Benefit first chose to set up business and the company moved up and down Sunbridge Road until they settled in premises at 12-14 Sunbridge Road in the 1890s. Once established, the firm remained faithful to the town, setting up other branches that were still present in the late 1960s.*

51 *(left) The former company premises still stand on Sunbridge Road, Bradford (in the centre of the photograph).*

3 Architectural Ornaments in the Neighbourhood

In the 1890s strong competition in the trade came from Freeman Hardy and Willis Limited (FH&W), a footwear group that over the years became a household name. Documents of the time show that FH&W began buying and registering business names that sounded uncannily similar to the Public Benefit Boot and Shoe Company. In an apparent threat to the Public Benefit branch opened by Franklin in Britton Ferry, FH&W opened branches at Haverford West and Tenby, trading under the name of Mutual Benefit Boot Company. This was an established company that had been bought by FH&W. Mutual Benefit Boot Company operated a small number of shops and had their headquarters perilously close to Public Benefit's Birmingham base headed by Benjamin Hunn.

The heat was on and the threat from FH&W seems to have drawn Franklin and Lennard into closer cooperation. The two had worked together since the early 1880s when Henry Lennard of Lennard Brothers managed a prestigious Public Benefit branch in Bristol. Lennard met the threat from FH&W's Mutual Benefit Boot Company by registering the similar-sounding business name of Mutual Boot Stores. The company registered a trademark showing a ship on the high seas and the slogan 'Let's pull together' suggesting that Lennard and Franklin were collaborating in an effort to defeat the invader.

52 Around the turn of the century Public Benefit opened a branch in the important Berkshire town of Reading – at 27 Broad Street. This view looking west down Broad Street, shows the premises on the corner of Queen Victoria Street (on the right, the corner closest to the camera). In 1903 the company moved across the street to 90 Broad Street and again in 1916 they moved to 95 Broad Street where the business continued to trade, but under the Lennards name for many years.

53 Advertisement that appeared in the Hull Daily Mail *in May 1889 reminding people that the company was 'British and Foreign Gold Medallists' and 'England's Chief Manufacturing Retailers'.*

The emergence of Mutual Boot Stores was countered by FH&W registering the business name of Peoples Benefit Boot Stores. This was a newly created company registered with the signatures of several employees, mainly clerks. The new company's headquarters were registered at Winchester House, 1 Welford Road, Leicester—a stone's throw from the Lennard's base. This jockeying for positions must have been the talk of the trade. War, it seems, had been declared! This last business name was never actually used by FH&W and registration was later discontinued, but the frantic registration manoeuvres show the level of concern and intense rivalry that was developing in the boot trade.

Documents from the early 1890s show that formal moves towards incorporation were under way. The name Public Benefit Boot Company Limited was registered in 1890 but by 1892 no allotment of shares had been made in the company. At this time the company was still in the process of acquiring additional businesses but formal transference of these businesses had yet to take place. The blatant threat from FH&W and others could very well have prompted the decision to rush through the registration of the company name at this time. As the company had become such a huge concern, it was imperative that the name was afforded protection from imitators and rivals who sought a larger share of the market.

The original Public Benefit Boot Company Limited from the 1890 attempt at incorporation was

---

DISTINGUISHED SUPREMACY.

PUBLIC BENEFIT BOOT COMPANY
PROSPECT - STREET HULL.
UNLIMITED AND UNPARALLELED

AUTUMN SUPPLIES.

THE MOST ADVANCED ENGLISH AND CONTINENTAL NOVELTIES AND SPECIALTIES.
ORDINARY AND UNCOMMON VARIETIES FOR PARTICULAR AND GENERAL WEAR.
PERFECTION IN STYLE, FORM, FIT, AND MAKE, OUTSTRIP PRAISE.

LADIES' SALOONS, GENTLEMEN'S SECTION, GENERAL DEPARTMENTS.

Comprehensive Collections of GOOD, BETTER, and BEST QUALITIES, at Prices to suit any desired outlay. The

SIX WINDOW EXPOSITIONS SHOW INCOMPARABLE VALUE,
READY-MADE AND CONSTRUCTED TO ORDER.
COLOURED BOOTS AND SHOES ARE FASHIONABLE FOR ALL PURPOSES.
MAKING to MEASURE is a very Large Business with the Company.
ACCURATE FIT and FAULTLESS MAKE in any Style. Consistent Prices.
REPAIRS are done equal to the Very Best New Work.
Inspection of Window Exhibits will Interest and give Desirable Information.

LADIES' SALOON ENTRANCE—ALBION-STREET.
GENTLEMEN'S SECTION, SEPARATE ENTRANCE—PROSPECT-STREET.
GENERAL DEPARTMENT, MAIN ENTRANCE—PROSPECT-STREET.

British and Foreign Gold Medallists. England's Chief Manufacturing Retailers.

GENERAL BRANCHES—HOLDERNESS-ROAD, HESSLE-ROAD, PORTER-STREET.

PUBLIC BENEFIT BOOT COMPANY.

54 Lennard Brothers trademark registered on 29 April 1885 by Lennard Brothers of 85 Asylum Street, Leicester.

55 Mutual Stores trademark registered on 29 April 1894 by Lennard Brothers, Leicester.

56 In 1906 Public Benefit's St Austell branch was located on the left side of this street at 32 Fore Street and in 1916 they moved to the other side at 15 Fore Street. Oliver's boot shop is on the left and another boot shop is evident on the other side of the road. Because it has not been possible to date this photograph with certainty, the precise whereabouts of the Public Benefit premises is unknown but they were in this vicinity of Fore Street for some decades.

57 In 1897 Public Benefit opened a store at 25 High Street, Barnstaple (opposite Cross Street and near to the corner of Butchers' Row). The photograph shows the shop's ornate lampshades and hanging carrier bags that are embellished with the well-known trademark – the horse, cart and boot. Public Benefit traded here until 1919 after which the company continued to trade, but under the Lennards' name. A rival boot shop, Oliver's, is evident further along the street at no.20.

liquidated and a new Public Benefit Boot Company Limited emerged in 1893. This latest incorporation formally brought together the business interests of William and George Franklin with those of Jabez Harker, Benjamin Hunn and the Dickinson and Kirby brothers. In the same year the company also bought out a quality ladies' footwear manufactory in Wellingborough.

With the merger, the newly incorporated Public Benefit enterprise now officially boasted two major factories and 40 branches, not including the seven or eight branches set up jointly by the Lennards and Franklins. The incorporation was also a precedent to a far greater amalgamation that was to take place in 1897.

Major expansion continued throughout the 1890s when new stores were opened at an astonishing rate. Advertisements in the *Stockton and Thornaby Herald* and the *South Durham Advertiser* in the early 1890s show branches operating at Stockton, Thornaby, Middlesbrough, West Hartlepool and Darlington. Advertisements in Loughborough in 1895 and 1896 reminded the readers of some of the larger branches:

Our establishments in Hull, Sheffield, Bristol, Belper, Ilkseton, Wakefield,

58 Taken from Cross Street, this photograph shows the Barnstaple branch (with the canopy) at the end of the street. The windows are well stocked and boots hang outside the shop. It may well be the manager posing in the shop doorway.

59 In Gainsborough, the company occupied premises in Heaton Street from around 1882. Early in the 1890s they moved to the prominent corner of Market Place and Silver Street, depicted here, where they remained for around 70 years.

60 The company occupied premises at19 Stall Street, Bath, for at least 40 years. This scene shows Stall Street around 1907. With the change in trading name from Public Benefit to Lennards, the branch site subsequently became known as Lennards Corner.

61 Advertisement that appeared in the Stockton & Thornaby Herald and South Durham Advertiser *on 10 November 1894.*

62 A notice in the Stockton & Thornaby Herald and South Durham Advertiser *on 29 February 1896 announced new closing times: ' – four nights a week at 7.30 p.m. and 10.30 p.m. on Saturday nights'.*

STILL ON THE WARPATH!
THORNABY TO BE CAPTURED!!

THE PUBLIC BENEFIT BOOT CO., LTD.,
Have OPENED PREMISES at

50, MANDALE-ROAD, 50
THORNABY-ON-TEES,

Thus enabling the residents to secure all the

ADVANTAGES IN PRICES AND QUALITIES
of the leading towns in

Don't be misled by LOW-PRICED RUBBISH, which is dear at any price. look for GENUINE ECONOMY and value from the

"PUBLIC BENEFIT."

STOCKTON : 144, HIGH-STREET (Opposite the Old Church).
THORNABY : 50, MANDALE-ROAD.
MIDDLESBROUGH : 44, LINTHORPE-ROAD.
WEST HARTLEPOOL : 78, LYNN-STREET.
DARLINGTON : 19, HIGH-ROW.
AND ALL OVER THE COUNTRY.

IMPORTANT NOTICE!

ALTERATION IN THE HOURS OF CLOSING.

THE PUBLIC BENEFIT BOOT CO., LTD.
Have decided to Close their Establishments on and after Monday, Feb. 3, as follows :—

MONDAY - - - 7.30 P.M. THURSDAY - - - 1. 0 P.M.
TUESDAY - - - 7.30 „ FRIDAY - - - 7.30 „
WEDNESDAY - - - 7.30 „ SATURDAY - - - 10.30 „

THE "PUBLIC BENEFIT"
CONFIDENTLY APPEAL TO THE PUBLIC TO

SHOP EARLY
AND THUS SUPPORT THEM IN THIS MUCH NEEDED REFORM

PUBLIC BENEFIT BOOT CO., LTD.,
144, HIGH-STREET (OPPOSITE THE OLD CHURCH), STOCKTON,
50, MANDALE-ROAD, THORNABY.

Loughborough, etc. The Company is the largest boot manufacturer in Great Britain, their goods are made to wear, and every pair is sold at wholesale prices.

The opening of a new East Hull branch in Holderness Road was given prominent editorial attention in the *Hull Times* of 27 June 1896:

What is described as an 'extraordinary event' in the improvement and development of East Hull takes place today when the Public Benefit Boot and Shoe Company's new and extensive premises in Holderness Road are to be opened.

A *Mail* representative has been personally conducted over the building, and the various departments, stock rooms, etc, brought to view by the courteous manager, afforded an interesting insight into the *modus operandi* of manufacturer dealing direct with the public, and the saving to the latter thereby effected. An advertisement in another column will convey some idea of the magnitude of the Public Benefit Boot and Shoe Company's operations. The building now opened in Holderness Road, immediately opposite the company's old premises and fronting the Presbyterian Church, is a very spacious structure, and an architectural ornament to the neighbourhood.

As an instance of an enterprising spirit in the improvement and development of East Hull, that under notice cannot be over estimated. In going over the new premises our representative was

63 *The Bedford Palace stands on the left-hand corner of this view of High Street, Bedford. The next building at 62 High Street is where Public Benefit commenced trading around 1910. For more than 60 years they occupied these premises – for most of that time trading under the Lennards' name. A large Lennards' sign can be seen high on this building.*

64 *Lennards opened a branch in picturesque Ilfracombe around the turn of the century and traded there for many decades.*

65 Illustration from an editorial item appearing in the Hull Times on 27 June 1896. This branch replaced small cramped premises on the opposite side of the road. The large structure had been in existence for many years prior to the company renovating it. The building experienced major alterations to suit the Public Benefit Boot Company business needs.

66 Below: Notable features of the Holderness Road branch included a striking clock and a series of sculptured boots and shoes. The latter, only to be seen by those with a keen eye and a yen for looking skyward, are on the façade.

struck with the magnitude of the undertaking, indicated by the numerous stock rooms and the various styles and classes of boots and shoes. All classes are, apparently, catered for, and fitting rooms of the most elaborate character are provided for the comfort and convenience of the company's customers—an important element in a vast concern. The new premises have been fitted with electric light (Crompton's Patent), of the company's own production, under the superintendence of Mr H.S. Tadman, electrical engineer, Hull, the engine, a 4 h.p., having been supplied by the well-known firm of engineers, Messrs Crossley and Company, Limited, Manchester. The builders were Messrs Hockney and Liggins, Witham; the signwork was executed by Mr Panton, Anlaby Road; the painting by Mr Hilken, Hedon Road; the plumbing by Mr Beal, Holderness Road; and the architect was Mr A. Gelder.

The whole of the work, it will thus be seen, has been executed by local people. Today's event may, therefore, be regarded as a red-letter day in the history of East Hull, an event which the *Mail* representative learned was looked forward to with very considerable interest by the residents of that populace. The building is no doubt a striking architectural ornament to East Hull. In front of it is a double-faced clock, electrically lighted, and guaranteed Greenwich time. This is sure to prove a great boon to the inhabitants of the district.

The company's advertisement in the same issue of the *Hull Times* gave further information about the 'most conspicuous building on Holderness Road':

Business had much outgrown the room of old shop, spacious premises in the most central position were purchased, partly re-built, enlarged, and transformed into a grand first-class and general mart, arranged to privately and openly serve large numbers at once, and hold stocks enough to supply all East Hull …

… Public Benefit Boot Company have now put East Hull on a par with Central Hull, by having a large replete and complete emporium conducted on the method of their British and Foreign Boot Exchange, Prospect Street. Those who have not done business with them because they could not be expeditiously served in the 'Old Limited Room Shop' will be promptly and satisfactorily supplied. They feel sure of adding thousands of new customers who are asked to kindly speak to friends of what they may purchase.

Special provision for window inspection. Large private space without impeding the footpath. At all times and seasons the window exhibits will be grand shows of superior varieties. Window exhibits will be great shows of extra special value.

The Holderness Road branch in East Hull was also featured in the *Illustrated Hull* at the time:

67 *Advertisement from the* Hull Times *of 27 June 1896 describes the premises as the 'most conspicuous building on Holderness Road.'*

The Holderness Road Branch is also one of the smartest and largest shops in East Hull, and was built in the latter part of 1896, the old establishment on the other side of the road being found inadequate to cope with the constantly increasing trade. As in Prospect Street, this shop is fitted up in the highest style of decoration, and is one of the sights of the East end. A large gas engine on the premises generates the electric light with which the building is so well illuminated.

George Franklin continued the challenge of developing business in Derby, using that town as a base from which to move into neighbouring towns. The Franklins were keen Wesleyans and commissioned John Wills, a Derby architect who specialised in Methodist chapels, to design the new Derby branch. Wills had designed new Public Benefit premises in Hull some years earlier. John Wills, who had flourished as an architect over the previous 30 years, was a specialist in acoustics and had gained himself a nationwide reputation designing many chapels and schools as well as some housing and commercial premises.

68 The recently refurbished company premises on Holderness Road, Hull, look good a century after the Public Benefit Boot Company opened for business in 1896.

In Derby, permission was obtained to demolish a tumbling Jacobean manor house that had been converted into shop units. It was situated on the prominent

69 The Metropole branch in the Babington Buildings, Derby, was the base for Public Benefit Boot Company activities in the region for many years. The building still stands proudly on the corner of Babington Lane and St Peter's Street. In this photograph it is the building on the extreme right with the lamps and canopies.

corner of Babbington Lane and St Peter's Street and it was on this site that Franklin built the brand new all-purpose Metropole branch that was opened around 1900. The new building design was broadly based on design elements, including the turrets, from the demolished house. Named the Babbington Buildings, the premises remained important throughout the history of the company.

The Franklin's Public Benefit Boot Company Limited that had been originally incorporated in 1890, then again in 1893, was liquidated and merged into the Public Benefit Boot Company Limited that was incorporated for the final time in 1897.

The assets brought into the amalgamation consisted of 51 branches in 37 towns including:

(a) William Franklin's three large purpose-built stores in Hull and numerous other stores including Wakefield, Gainsborough and Castleford; Beverley, York, Goole, Doncaster, Grantham, Mexborough, Normanton, Morley, Barton on Humber and Wainfleet;

(b) George Franklin's Metropole in Derby along with branches in Belper, Ripley, Ilkeston, Loughborough, Retford and Uttoxeter;

(c) George Franklin and Benjamin Hunn's large premises at 42 Corporation Street, Birmingham along with five other branches and a store in Walsall;

(d) Jabez Harker's prominent Albert Hall Buildings in Nottingham and a store at Newark;

70 *In this 1906 photograph of St Peter's Street, Derby, the company's premises can be seen on the corner just to the left of the light pole. Part of the building was let to the Raleigh Cycle Co for many years.*

71 *The Babington Buildings still form part of a busy shopping precinct in the heart of Derby.*

72 *Door detail on the Babington Buildings, Derby.*

(e) John Kirby's prestigious store at the Moorhead in Sheffield, four other Sheffield branches plus one store at Chesterfield;

(f) George Kirby's successful stores at Warrington and Widnes;

(g) Brow Dickinson's factories at Bramley and Wellingborough and branches across the North East including Stockton, Middlesbrough, Redcar, Thornaby, West Hartlepool, Hartlepool, two branches in Bradford and three branches in Leeds.

The formal notice of the General Meeting to present the accounts regarding the company merger and new incorporation appeared in the *London Gazette*, 9 August 1898:

The Public Benefit Boot Company Limited
(Incorporated in 1893)

Notice is hereby given that in pursuance of section 142 of the Companies Act 1862 a General Meeting of the Member of the above named Company will be held at No. 39 Park-place in the city of Leeds on Monday the 12th day of September 1898 at 1.15 o'clock in the afternoon for the purpose of having an account laid before them showing the manner in which the winding up has been conducted and the property of the Company disposed of and of hearing any explanation that may be given by the Liquidator and also of determining by Extraordinary Resolution the manner in which the books, accounts and documents of the Company and of the Liquidator shall be disposed of.—Dated the eighth day of August 1898.

Walter Charlton, Liquidator.

N.B.—This Company was merged in the Public Benefit Boot Company Limited incorporated in 1897.

Interestingly, some footwear retailers of the day possessed far more branches than Public Benefit, but concentrated on a single area such as London, thereby reducing problems in logistics and supply. Public Benefit, on the other hand, had infiltrated large areas of the country and continued that tactic aggressively. Although more difficult to achieve, the strategy was potentially far more rewarding and there were the benefits of not putting all the eggs in one basket.

The grand opening of William Franklin's new purpose-built store on the corner of Coltman Street and Hessle Road, Hull was announced with appropriate fanfare in the *Hull Times* on 9 October 1897:

To the inhabitants West End, Dairycoates, South Newington, Hessle, etc. 'Tis well known that for eleven years, we, Public Benefit Boot Company, have done most of the district's boot and shoe trade at Wellsted Street corner, Hessle Road. Its rapid growth and prospective immense increase forced us to erect a capacious building with facilities to unlimitedly develop it. In the most central, commanding position, Coltman Street corner, Hessle Road, we have built, as the press describes:

A colossal, magnificent structure of architectural elegance, handsomely and substantially fitted and furnished, electrically lit with own plant on best method. Four large exposition windows, immense sale shop, ladies' and gentlemen's fitting departments, and stock-rooms fixtured to hold hundreds of thousands of pairs. Brightly illuminated public clock—Greenwich time—a great acquisition

73 *Illustration from an advertisement in the* Hull Times *of 9 October 1897 announcing the opening of the new Public Benefit Boot Company premises on the corner of Hessle Road and Coltman Street, Hull. This important extension of the company's presence in Hull replaced inadequate premises nearby. The purpose-built prestige store attracted enormous trade over the years. It was frequented by thousands of workers in the nearby fishing industry – seamen, fish factory workers, dock-workers and men working in allied industries in this part of town. Designed by leading architect Alfred Gelder, the building is remarkably similar in appearance to the Doncaster branch opened a year later.*

74 *In 1925 the Hessle Road branch was sold to the Co-operative Society and today the building has been magnificently refurbished by the current owners, Malcolm and Ian Shields of Premier Workwear.*

75 *In 1888 the Public Benefit Boot Company had their Midlands headquarters based in the 'workshop of the world' – Birmingham. This magnificent branch at 42 Corporation Street stood proud amongst a range of equally lofty structures, banks and various business houses – all reflecting the great wealth generated by this industrialised city. At the time there was also another store at 21-23 Union Street. By 1897, in addition to having their main branch in Corporation Street, there were branches at 71 Longmore Street, 22 Union Street, 78 Lichfield Road, 186 Coventry Road and 61 Spring Hill. The company continued to trade in Birmingham and region up until at least the mid-1970s.*

THE PUBLIC BENEFIT BOOT Co., LTD.,

MANUFACTURING RETAILERS
DIRECT FROM FACTORY TO PEOPLE

to the district and an ornament to the road. All classes will, no doubt, be proud of it, and congratulate themselves on having one of the largest and best fitted general boot and shoe marches in the Empire, a companion edifice to the company's gigantic concern, Prospect Street, and new large establishment, Holderness Road. We predict for the Hessle Road 'Boot Palace' the enormous business which all communities naturally expected, and so fully prepared for. The opinions of a few faint-hearted or envious traders—'It's too big,' 'far too good for the district,' will prove to be weak-knee judgement, the company's enterprise and success may probably incite chiefs in other business to follow suit. True to their principle of supporting home production and labour in the cities and towns they erect shops, Hessle Road building was designed and constructed by Hull workmen, and as far as possible, with city materials. This example of 'home employment' is worthy of emulation. 'Tis evident the President and Directors of the Public Benefit Boot Company Limited, have strongest confidence in the solid progression of Hull, the extension and trade advancement of the city's main shipping and fishing districts—their faith is ours. We understand Saturday October 9th is 'Opening Day' of this extraordinary marche.

The year of Queen Victoria's Diamond Jubilee, 1897, also saw the amalgamation of the partnerships and assets of Thomas Lennard with those of his brother John Lennard. Also signing the agreement were J.W. Goddard (manufacturing chemist), G. Chattaway (boot manufacturer) and R. Walker (gentleman).

At this time Thomas Lennard made a pact with Franklin and the recently incorporated Public Benefit enterprise. Lennard would allow all of the newly acquired branches purchased from his brother Samuel to trade under the Public

76 This 1920s view was taken from New Street, looking north up Corporation Street, Birmingham. The Public Benefit premises stood on the corner of Corporation Street and Union Street, a short distance up the street on the right.

77 An early view of Lennards Limited headquarters with its turret and flagpole. The building was located at the junction of Triangle West and Queen's Road, Bristol. Like many of the other company's corner locations it became known as 'Lennards Corner'. Along with the Triangle cinema, the Lennards headquarters were destroyed in an air raid on 24 November 1940. The site was cleared in 1955 and a Maples store arose a year later.

78 This typical Lennards Limited advertisement from the early 1900s depicted their headquarters and promoted 'All-British' boots and shoes.

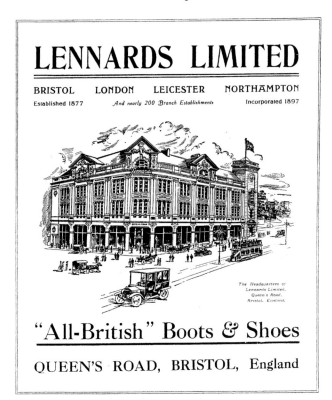

Benefit name as they had operated in Bristol and Leicester—and then mark out specific territories over which his company would exercise control.

The effect of this was a dramatic increase in the number of new branches opened within these delineated territories. All of the branches traded under the common name of Public Benefit Boot Company but were controlled and managed by Lennard. From 1897 this gentlemen's agreement to respect individual borders, sparked an era of co-operation characterised by rapid advancement and a frantic rush to establish new territories ahead of any rivals.

All branches were opened in one of three ways—either solely by Franklin, solely by Lennard, or as a joint venture. Thomas Lennard, Chairman and Managing Director of Lennards Limited, was also afforded the option to buy any premises within his territories that he did not already wholly or partially own.

Lennard drew his broad territorial lines to include Devon, Cornwall, the Home Counties, Wales, the South Coast, London and of course Bristol and Leicester. These were all areas where William Franklin had previously begun to make inroads. In 1897 a total of 25 branches were opened in these territories.

Lennard also acquired land on a prestigious site in Queens Road, Bristol, on which to build their large headquarters. Here he centralised all Lennards' administration, distribution, manufacture and warehousing operations.

In March 1898 an advertisement in *The Doncaster Gazette* announced the opening of new Public Benefit premises in Doncaster:

> The talk of Doncaster and villages for miles around. History of Doncaster will record in its trading annals this extraordinary dedicatory opening event of the town's finest commercial building, Public Benefit Boot Company's Limited, Majestic Boot and Shoe Marche!

79 *An advertisement from* The Gazette Doncaster Directory, *1903*

80 *Looking down Printing Office Street from St Sepulchre Gate in the early 1900s with The Public Benefit Boot Company building on the left hand corner.*

81 *Illustration of the company's new Doncaster premises on the corner of Printing Office Street and St Sepulchre Gate, published in the* Doncaster Gazette, *March 1898.*

82 *The old company building continues to be an attractive landmark in a still busy trading area of Doncaster – close to the town market.*

83 *The Public Benefit windows of the Doncaster branch on the right are jammed full of merchandise. Trams trundle down Station Road towards the railway station. Development over the years has seen Station Road disappear and the Frenchgate Centre shopping precinct has replaced it.*

84 Kirkgate in Wakefield as depicted in a watercolour painting by Ethel J. Hein. Public Benefit established a branch on Kirkgate in the early 1880s and quickly flourished, setting up in three locations on Kirkgate until 1898 when they erected a grand emporium on the same street.

85 Advertisement depicting the company's new building in Market Street, York, published in the Yorkshire Gazette *in 1902.*

86 Advertisement for 'Great Removal Sale' as the company prepares to vacate its premises in Clifford Street prior to their move to Market Street, York.

Public Opinion: A great acquisition—Enterprise deserving universal support—Town improvement—Architectural street adornment—Grand concern—Splendid place—Magnificent building—Extraordinary edifice—Great boon tower clock—Precisely what Doncaster wanted—Courageous undertaking—Statue of the company's national trading greatness.

A new, larger branch, alongside the old Public Benefit shop in Kirkgate, Wakefield, also opened in October 1898. At the time Wakefield had a population of around 23,000 and was a prosperous market town, benefiting from being on the border of the textile towns to the west, and the coal mining villages and farming communities to the south and east. In an advertisement announcing the new Wakefield branch, the manager Jonathan Rose enthused about the new premises and appointments:

Wakefield's Wondrous Palace Marche Mansion Emporium. Built to best serve all communities. Tremendous Trade Opening Day. Saturday October 14. Public Benefit Boot Co.'s Ltd New Mammoth Marche (adjoining old shop) Kirkgate, Wakefield. Capable of stocking half-million pairs. Bright electric-lit public clock—Brilliantly electrically illuminated—Grand sights—Three huge window exhibitions—Qualities, varieties that have won First Prize Gold Medals against all England—Largest cities have not a more complete and replete Boot-Shoe Marche—Call for Bill of Opening if not received—View grand window expositions—splendid Marche—Ladies Saloon—Gentlemen's Section—General Divisions.

The 1902 opening of the new Public Benefit premises in Market Street, York, was rated as a 'stupendous success!!' A week or so after the opening, a company

STUPENDOUS SUCCESS!!
IMMENSE OPENING BUSINESS.

Great Trade Daily from All Classes. Crowds of Window Viewers all day long. Buyers come from Surrounding Towns and Villages.

PUBLIC BENEFIT BOOT COMPANY'S
Grand Central Majestic Marche,
MARKET STREET.

GREATEST BUILDING IMPROVEMENT YORK HAS HAD FOR MANY YEARS.
YORK EQUALS LONDON NOW WITH A COMPLETE BOOT EMPORIUM.

PUBLIC BENEFIT BOOT COMPANY, Market Street, YORK.

PUBLIC BENEFIT BOOT CO.
GREAT REMOVAL SALE
Commenced FRIDAY, JANUARY 3rd.

The whole of our Immense Stock of HIGH-CLASS **BOOTS AND SHOES**
Will be cleared out previous to removing to our New Central Premises in Market Street.

See Windows on Saturday! Buy there on Saturday! Stupendous Reductions!

About 800 pairs of LADIES' SATIN SHOES, All Fresh and Clean, All Colors, 1/6 to 1/11½ per pair.

See Windows! Fresh Bargains each Day! Come at once and secure the Best Bargains!

PUBLIC BENEFIT BOOT CO., CLIFFORD ST., YORK.

advertisement highlighted the distinct departments—ladies' saloon, gentlemen's section and general division. The small print told more of the story:

Public Benefit Boot Company's thirteen years' enormous trade in Clifford Street made with city and country people, of all societies, by selling sterling superior qualities, desirable varieties, charging honest prices, giving better wear-value than obtainable anywhere in the city at same cost, supplying working people

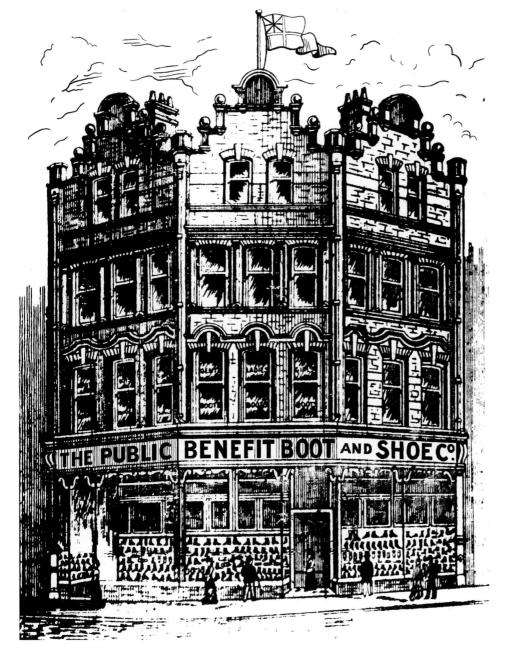

87 A 1902 illustration used to advertise the opening of Public Benefit's 'Grand Central Majestic Marche' in Market Street, York.

88 A contemporary photograph of the Market Street premises, still very much in use.

89 *Watched over by two male supervisors, women busy themselves in the Closing Room in a well-appointed footwear factory. It has not been possible to determine if these particular sewing machines were powered by gas, steam or pedal.*

90 *Clicking department around the 1890s with rolls of leather on a weighing machine in the foreground. Lighting is by both natural daylight and gaslight.*

91 Around 1899 Public Benefit opened premises at 139 High Street, Poole, and they continued trading on this street for at least three decades. The store is on the extreme right of this photograph and the horse-drawn boot trademark is clearly visible on the row of hanging lampshades outside the shop. This was one of many branches whose ownership within the group and trading name changed a number of times. Over the years the branch traded variously under the name of Lennard Bros, Public Benefit, and finally Lennards Ltd.

the most durable, serviceable boots, shoes that can be made, suiting everybody with what they want, what they fancy, what they like.

Country buyers visiting York should see the window shows, and buy in this great marche. City purchasers of all classes should view the window shows, and buy in this great marche.

Whatever's wanted—black, tan, brown, chrome; boots, shoes; for adults, youngsters; Whatever's needed in shape, style, make, size, sort, quality, any kind, boots, shoes, The place to get uttermost wearworth at fairest prices. Public Benefit Boot Company, Market Street, York.

92 The company's Rotherham premises in the distinctive Imperial Buildings can be seen up the street on a distant corner in this view.

From 1897 to 1905 new branch openings had continued feverishly but the Franklin group still had many more branches than those opened by the Lennards. A concerted effort was made to achieve equal status and to break down the old territorial boundaries and develop the culture of a true partnership.

While the process of opening new branches continued unabated, a merger between the Franklin group and the Lennards group of Bristol had become a real prospect. However, such a merger was never going to be easy and was dependent on the full cooperation of the various members of the boards and that simply did not occur. The idea of an equal merger was probably conceived at the time of the 1897 agreement when the two distinct trading territories were set up.

Put Your Foot In It.

That's the way to tell the real character of a Boot. You can't judge a Boot in a shop window.

When you try on one of our half-guinea Boots, you will notice it conform to every line of the foot. When you stand, your foot spreads, and this Boot is made to spread with it. It is the most wonderful line of Boots in the Kingdom —made in Ladies' and Gentlemen's—in the most fashionable styles—and made after a careful study of the human foot. Popular price, 10/6.

Four Convenient Shops.

PUBLIC BENEFIT BOOT COMPANY,

Prospect-st.   Anlaby-rd.
Holderness-rd.   Hessle-rd.

Football Talk.

The kicking is a considerable part of the game; and the boots are a considerable factor in the kicking.

A good deal depends upon the running; and the running largely depends upon the boots.

When you reckon it all up, the boots are responsible for much of the game.

Have them right.

A splendid range of Football Boots awaits you here, in Chrome, Russet, and all prevailing styles. We study Footballers' needs, and offer specialities that will interest you. Prices 4/11½ to 10/6.

Four Convenient Shops.

PUBLIC BENEFIT BOOT COMPANY,

Prospect-st.   Anlaby-rd.
Holderness-rd.   Hessle-rd.

All Boots Look Alike

when they are new. It is when they get into actual wear —when the top polish is taken off, that the real boots show themselves.

The Public Benefit Company's Boots are honestly made inside as well as outside. The unseen parts are as carefully executed as the final polishing for the window display. That's why our Boots give good results and absolute satisfaction. The new Autumn styles are now on show.

Four Convenient Shops.

PUBLIC BENEFIT BOOT COMPANY,

Prospect-st.   Anlaby-rd.
Holderness-rd.   Hessle-rd.

Shabby Boots.

A pair of shabby Boots will completely spoil the effect of an otherwise well-dressed man. Yet you may often notice it. In most cases it is an oversight. A man is apt to think his boots "don't matter." Smart Boots are essential to well-dressed men.

We sell the most wonderful line of half-guinea business Boots in the kingdom. Real smart, well-finished, well turned-out Boots. They are made in all the various leathers at present in fashion, with broad, medium, and narrow toes. At the popular price—10/6.

Four Convenient Shops.

PUBLIC BENEFIT BOOT COMPANY,

Prospect-st.   Anlaby-rd.
Holderness-rd.   Hessle-rd.

After the Holidays

We are specialists in complete Footwear Outfits for School. Every requirement is here provided for in the fullest possible manner. School Boots and Shoes for ordinary wear— Football Boots—Walking and Running Shoes—Slippers—and every other kind of footwear for young ladies and gentlemen. Honest materials and honest workmanship at prices that are consistently low.

Four Convenient Shops.

PUBLIC BENEFIT BOOT COMPANY,

Prospect-st.   Anlaby-rd.
Holderness-rd.   Hessle-rd.

Do You Dance ?

Our beautiful exhibition of Dress Shoes, for Ladies, Gentlemen, and Children, will interest every one who dances, and many who do not. The whole stock is characterised by good taste. It charms all who see it.

These Dress Shoes are the best value to be found anywhere. The styles are taken from the latest and best models. And as for the prices—they range from 1/11½ to 21/-.

Four Convenient Shops.

PUBLIC BENEFIT BOOT COMPANY,

Prospect-st.   Anlaby-rd.
Holderness-rd.   Hessle-rd.

93 Series of advertisements published in the Hull News *in 1906. The advertising campaign was a departure from the kind of advertising used previously by the company.*

Good Value, Too !

Not only is our half-guinea boot a most comfortable, and a most sensible piece of footwear—it is also exceptional value. Imagine a boot put together in such a way that it conforms to every line of the foot; that it spreads and contracts naturally with the foot as you walk. Such a boot can be obtained elsewhere— but it usually costs 16/6. Here it is at the popular price 10/6. It is made for Ladies and Gentlemen, in the newest leathers, in black and brown. You can see it in the windows.

Four Convenient Shops.

PUBLIC BENEFIT BOOT COMPANY,

Prospect-st.   Anlaby-rd.
Holderness-rd.   Hessle-rd.

Outdoor Workers.

All outdoor workers, such as Postmen, Policemen, Tram Drivers and Conductors, need to wear sound Boots. It is not generally known that the best possible leather for bad weather, lime, and chemicals is Chrome Calf. For all purposes that require hard wear this leather is without equal. The Public Benefit "Long Service" Brand is made of Chrome Calf, in Black and Brown. This is an excellent Boot for outdoor workers— made in four shapes at **10/9**

Four Convenient Shops.

PUBLIC BENEFIT BOOT COMPANY,

Prospect-st.   Anlaby-rd.
Holderness-rd.   Hessle-rd.

Mere Boot Sellers

should not be entrusted with the fitting of your feet. A pair of badly fitting boots may, in a short time, permanently injure your foot.

Our Half-guinea Boot is the most wonderful line in the kingdom. It is built to conform to every line of the foot —built so that it adapts itself to the foot, instead of adapting the foot to the boot.

Made for Ladies and Gentlemen, in black and brown, at 10/6.

Four Convenient Shops.

PUBLIC BENEFIT BOOT COMPANY,

Prospect-st.   Anlaby-rd.
Holderness-rd.   Hessle-rd.

94 The Public Benefit shop at 379-380 High Street, Cheltenham is visible on the far right of this early 1900's postcard. The store, like many company premises, was situated in a busy thoroughfare. Typically, footwear can be seen stacked high in the windows and shoes with large white price tags attached, hanging on hooks outside the shop.

95 The style of promotional tin produced by the company around 1905.

96 In October 1910 Miss Lynch of Bream Lodge sent a postcard to the Public Benefit Boot Company branch in Cheltenham requesting that a footwear catalogue be sent to her.

Subtle differentiation was apparent in the naming of stores depending on whether they came under the umbrella of Leeds or Bristol management. The most obvious was naming the stores either *Public Benefit Boot Co* or *Public Benefit Boot Co (The)*. The use of *The* in brackets later became quite significant in identifying branches opened and managed by the northern-based Franklin board. Other examples of this particular identification were seen again in 1889 at Sheffield and also at the factory in Palk Road, Wellingborough. Another earlier variation on the title, *The Original Public Benefit Boot Co* was used when branches were opened at Stall Street, Bath in 1892 and at Frome in 1897. However, the latter two branches

97 *The company occupied premises at 30 Newborough (on the corner of King Street) in Scarborough for some decades from early in the century. In this photograph, the Public Benefit branch is on the right, just past the man driving a horse and cart. Scarborough castle can be seen in the distance. In Scarborough the company also traded at various locations on Westborough for almost 70 years.*

98 *Letterhead used by the company in the 1890s.*

did eventually come under the control of Lennards. In 1900 when four branches were opened in Lincolnshire, all were identified as *Public Benefit Boot Co (The)*. The same identification style was used in 1902 when branches opened in Barnstaple, Bideford, Exeter, Ilfracombe, East Stonehouse, Plymouth and Torquay — despite being in the heart of Lennard territory these branches were opened by the Franklin board of directors. This subtle way of distinguishing stores became quite commonplace and was again used in 1903 when four branches opened in Swindon and in 1907 when others emerged in Liverpool.

99 The company was based at 39 Park Place, Leeds in the 1890s until they moved their headquarters to much larger premises in 1904.

100 Public Benefit occupied two premises at Ripon – the first one at 18 Fishergate from around 1917. Ten years later they were located in the Ripon Market Place, pictured here.

101 Public Benefit had a branch at 60 Oldham Street in bustling Manchester from the 1890s and remained there for about 30 years. This branch was the headquarters for the Manchester region. The view of Oldham Street is from around 1906. A few years later the company had branches at 407 Oxford Road in Manchester and at 118-120 Stretford Road in Hulme and by 1929 seven stores were operating under the Lennards name in the Manchester area.

102 This view looking west down Boscawen Street, Truro, shows in the centre distance an imposing bank building on the corner of King Street. The Public Benefit premises, difficult to distinguish in this photo, were directly opposite the bank on the north-east corner of Boscawen Street and King Street. In June Palmer's 1994 book Edwardian Truro *she refers to the widening of King Street, Truro and the plans drawn up in 1906: for splendid new premises on the corner of King Street and Boscawen Street (the present site of the Midland bank) for the Public Benefit Boot Company, a national chain of shoe shops. These plans included offices, a sitting room, two w.c.s and a lavatory (probably for staff) on the first floor: and on the second floor, living quarters consisting of two bedrooms, dining room, kitchen, bathroom and separate w.c.*

103 In the early 1900s William Harker traded as a boot and shoe retailer at 42 Northgate Street in the ancient town of Chester. Around 1907 and for the following few decades, the business traded at the same address under the Public Benefit name. In 1927 a second Chester branch was opened on Foregate Street, pictured here some years earlier. A repair facility also operated at 5 Grosvenor Street. Chester was one of only a handful of company locations such as Hull, Stockton and Derby that offered specialist shoe repairs outside Leeds; they continued this repair service up into 1950s

104 The Public Benefit branch in Banbury began at 7 Parsons Street in 1899 and continued until it became Lennards Ltd during the Great War. In the 1920s Lennards abandoned Parsons Street in favour of a branch in the Market Place where it remained as 'Lennards Corner'. Banbury Market Place is a typically wide market street and the cattle pens are seen on the extreme right.

4 Manoeuvring in the New Century

From 1897 to 1904, many of the individual businesses that had amalgamated to form the Public Benefit corporation were largely run and controlled, as they had been previously, from offices and warehouses in Hull, Leeds, Birmingham, Warrington and Sheffield. It was apparent that the company was not capitalising on the full benefits of amalgamation, so a programme of reorganisation and centralisation commenced.

Throughout the 1890s the company's headquarters were at 39 Park Place in Leeds but in 1904 large premises were acquired nearby in St Paul's Street. St Paul's House had five floors and 63,000 square feet of floor space and was originally a factory and warehouse built in 1879 for a clothing magnate John Barran. The Moorish–Venetian style of the building was said to be inspired by the original owner's enthusiasm for the Doge's Palace that he had visited in Venice. The prolific Leeds architect Thomas Ambler, who was known for his singularly varied use of the mixed-Gothic and Renaissance styles, designed the building in 1878.

St Paul's House has a distinctive Venetian-Gothic character with its pointed arches, shafts and Italianate tracery heads to the windows. The façade consists of regular bays, with the windows to the ground and mezzanine floors united within

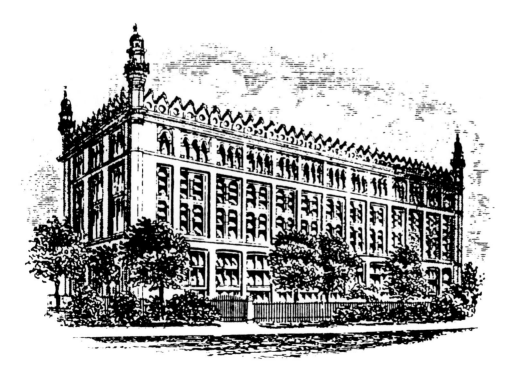

105 St Paul's House, Leeds, became the impressive new headquarters of the company in 1904.

106 *The company's headquarters from Park Square.*

107 *The early years of the 20th century were significant for The Public Benefit Boot Company as they moved into their large and prestigious headquarters in Leeds. Queen Victoria had died in 1901 and her loyal subjects paid tribute by erecting numerous memorials in cities throughout the country including, depicted here, Nottingham.*

108 *The architectural detail of this building continues to draw comment and admiration from people interested in the architectural heritage of this country.*

a frame of fine decorative terracotta. The first- and second-floor windows have a similar treatment and the third-floor windows have triple Moorish styled arches. Five dramatic terracotta minarets are featured on top of the slender octagonal towers at each of the five corners of the building. The building was designed as a model factory and warehouse and its flexible layout took into account the practical requirements of the new manufacturing processes. The building became a well-known Leeds landmark and still stands well preserved, proudly overlooking the elegant Park Square.

All operations were transferred to the impressive new headquarters in 1904 and the two manufacturing bases of Wellingborough and Bramley were closed down along with the various administrative sites at Hull, Birmingham, Derby, Sheffield and Warrington. No doubt it was with some reluctance that managers and directors had to release their individual power bases and embrace the new central ideal.

Lennard had successfully brought together his manufacturing and retailing in Bristol in 1897 but the widely scattered units run by the Franklins still had to work through the complexities of the centralisation process.

Prior to 1904 Public Benefit consisted of a series of territories controlled by a director of the company—each area with its own regional office. With the closure of the various regional offices and shifting of the power base to the new

109 One of the ornate entrances to St Paul's House.

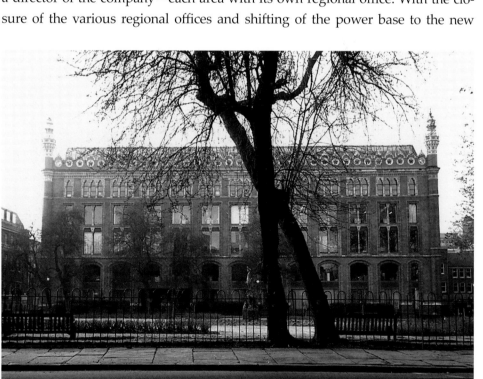

110 Built in 1879 but well preserved, the company's former headquarters still look majestically over Park Square, Leeds. It is now a Grade Two listed building.

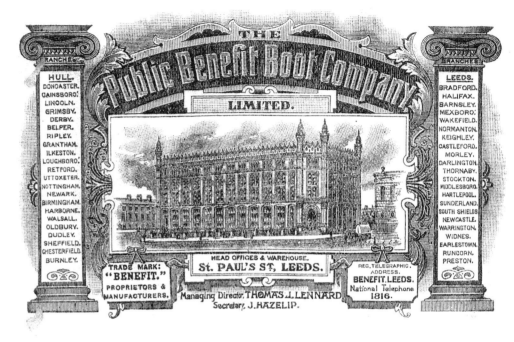

headquarters in Leeds, groups of small shops were placed under the control of senior managers. Whilst this arrangement worked up to a point, there may have occasionally been a lack of communication between head office and the shops as district inspectors were appointed to travel around a defined area. In some ways they were doing the job previously performed by the various founders, for example, John Kirby, who controlled all aspects of running the Sheffield and Chesterfield branches.

The district inspectors were men who apparently wielded considerable power, reporting only to the directors. Their responsibilities included the hiring and firing of staff, maintenance of premises and instructing staff on how best to organise the shop and present the merchandise. Some of the more highly regarded inspectors eventually went on to become directors of the company so it was possibly a career path that many aspired to. It is likely that some rivalry existed between the various district managers in competing for director status.

In 1904 we see the start of great upheaval within the company when Thomas Lennard was invited to join the Leeds board to begin implementation of the merger of the trading territories. The chief executives were Franklin who was based in Leeds and Lennard who had made his headquarters in Bristol. Yet, store ownership became an important issue as Lennard was disadvantaged to the point of not owning the same ratio of branches even in his own territories because of a late start. Once the merger was imminent, it was conceivable that everything should be equal. The new super-company would have a huge

112 Church Gate in Loughborough – a typical midland market town around the turn of the century. The Public Benefit Boot Company branch is on the left just past the shops with canopies. Boots and shoes with white price tags can be seen hanging on rails at the front.

113 This view of Queen Street, Cardiff, shows the Public Benefit shop on the left side of the street. The company went to great lengths to try to be different from their many rivals. They made liberal use of the company logo – the horse-drawn dray displaying the giant boot. In this Cardiff store the logo is used on the window blind at the top and also on the hanging exterior lights. Each of the lights has a square glass shade depicting the company trademark that would be fully illuminated once the lighting was turned on. There is the usual full fronted sign at the top of the building in case anyone is in any doubt that we have the Public Benefit Boot Co here. An ornate wrought-iron bracket holding the 'Buy Public Benefit Shoes' sign has a sculptured boot within the wrought iron and there is another symbol highlighted on the side wall of the building. It looks very much like a medal and could possibly have been some reference to the three gold medals the company attained at the Paris exhibition some years earlier.

potential for buying and retailing but, despite this extraordinary opportunity to expand, opposition was growing and rocky times lay ahead.

It appears that disagreements occurred in the boardroom a few months later when founder William Franklin resigned from the board along with the chairman Sir James Woodhouse and fellow solicitor Christopher Graham. This may have been a deliberate strategy on the part of the founder and chairman to force through the changes required to promote the advancement of a truly world-class, multiple footwear company. These resignations, however, did afford Thomas Lennard the chance to acquire not only a major stake holding but the opportunity to effect real influence and power on both boards of directors.

Lennard immediately raised the capital necessary to acquire the major shareholding from Franklin and the others and became chairman of the board and managing director, in the process ousting Brow Dickinson from his role as managing director. Also elected to the board at this time was another Lennard's man, Wallis Goddard.

A solution to the vexing question of inequality of assets was partly solved when Thomas Lennard acquired the shareholding of William Franklin and became chairman. He began a process of transferring his new assets to the control of his Bristol headquarters, thus achieving equal status. However, this solution

114 Public Benefit occupied premises at 79 St Mary Street, Cardiff at the turn of the century. This view of St Mary Street dates from around 1905. Nine years later all the Cardiff branches were trading under the Lennards' name.

115 Enamel advertising plate used around the turn of the century. These plates would have been displayed prominently on the interior and exterior walls of company premises.

116 Control of individual branches in 1905 by The Public Benefit Boot Company of Leeds and Lennards Limited of Bristol.

	PUBLIC BENEFIT BOOT CO LEEDS	LENNARDS LIMITED BRISTOL
Branches jointly controlled by Public Benefit Boot Co, Leeds and Lennards Ltd, Bristol	44	
Branches trading as Public Benefit Boot Co	56	
Branches trading as Public Benefit Boot Co (Lennards Ltd)		37
Branches transferred from Public Benefit Boot Co Leeds to Public Benefit Boot Co (Lennards Ltd)		17
Branches trading as Lennards Ltd		2
Total number of branches controlled by each company in 1905	100	100

117 Postcard of the Repairing Factory façade on Brook Street, Hull, postmarked 1906.

became a major issue with some directors on the boards in Leeds and Bristol. It would have undoubtedly upset Brow Dickinson and John Kirby—the strongest critics of the plan. John Lennard, the secretary of Lennards Limited, resigned, probably over the issue of amalgamation. Thomas Lennard, though, was not going to accept anything less than chairmanship and the managing directorship of the new enlarged company—being the major shareholder, he pressed ahead with his plans. An ambitious man, he was of a similar hardworking and innovative disposition as his counterpart William Franklin.

In 1905 a total of 17 stores were transferred from the control of the Leeds board to Bristol; this caused much consternation amongst some of the other

118 High Street, Yeovil, where the company traded firstly as The Public Benefit Boot Company and later as Lennards for some decades. The company traded in a dozen centres throughout Somerset.

directors who would have strongly opposed this idea. However the branches involved were all branches that William Franklin had personally had a hand in opening and came completely under Lennard's ownership when he took over Franklin's shareholding. These branches were Keighley, Barnsley, Castleford, Mexborough, Normanton, Doncaster, Wakefield, Halifax and Morley and two branches in Goole, making 11 branches in Yorkshire. Six branches were passed over from Lancashire—Burnley, Preston, Warrington, Newton-le-Willows and two branches in

119 In 1905 Public Benefit occupied premises at 75 St James Street in the Lancashire town of Burnley. In this view about 1911 the premises are in the building on the left where a gentleman on a ladder is adjusting the canopy. The textile industry made Burnley the world's largest cloth producer and Public Benefit catered for the needs of, amongst others, the mill and warehouse workers. The company maintained a presence in Burnley for the following 50 years.

Widnes. The idea of separate and distinguishable territories was starting to dis-integrate. The table on p.58 shows that, with the 1905 transfer of some branches, equality was achieved with Leeds and Bristol boards maintaining control of an equal number of branches.

Anxiety existed during this turbulent period when early in 1906 George Frank-lin followed the path of his brother William and also resigned his directorship—a very clear indication of the turbulent times in which they were operating.

From study of the few surviving company documents from this period, we gain an insight into the climate within the company when the merger was attempted. In February 1908 the next sudden resignation from the board is that of John Kirby. However, a few months later, in May 1908, Thomas Lennard also resigned and John Kirby was reinstated on the board and took up the chair-manship. Brow Dickinson was then reappointed managing director. Goddard remained on the board of both companies—perhaps the eyes and ears of Bristol-based Lennard who still hoped to implement plans for a merger. Due to the intricacies of store ownership up to and during this period, the merger looked as though it could be intact. There were new branches opening and stores continued to be transferred to the Bristol-based Lennards' control in a continuing effort to equalise the numbers.

The company literature does not document much of this activity so a degree of conjecture must be used. However, it was obviously a very turbulent period in the Leeds and Bristol boardrooms. The following excerpts from a surviving

Lennards' prospectus, dated 6 March 1909, gives insight into the company's operation at this time:

Lennards Limited
(Public Benefit Boot Company)
PROSPECTUS

Lennards Limited was formed in 1897 with a capital of £60,000 to acquire an old established business, the capital has since been increased to £120,000 and it is now proposed to increase it by another £30,000 making a total of £150,000; there are also £30,000 in 4% debentures. The business was founded by Mr T J Lennard, who has been Chairman and Managing Director for the last twelve years, and who has agreed to retain control for a further seven years at least. The Directors named on the front of this Prospectus have been Directors of the Company since its incorporation twelve years ago, so there has been no break in the continuity of control …

120 A large square sign on the left identifies this Swindon branch of The Public Benefit Boot Company on Regent Street where they traded from the 1890s. Over the years the company also occupied premises on Bridge Street, Fleet Street and Wood Street in Swindon.

121 Lennards had a long presence at 18 High Street, Stamford, Lincolnshire, from the early 1900s until the 1970s. Their premises were on the section of High Street depicted here; the street to the right is Ironmongers Street.

122 Drawings of Lennards' Bristol headquarters were used extensively in their advertisements.

123 *View looking north on High Street, Stockton-on-Tees, where the Public Benefit Boot Company established a presence as early as 1880 when they were located at 152 High Street. By 1896 they opened a purpose-built store at 144 High Street, opposite the church. From 1920 to the 1970s Public Benefit traded at 135 High Street. Stockton-on-Tees remained an important distribution and repair centre for the company for many years.*

124 *Postcard dated 1910 of the branch at 144 High Street, Stockton-on-Tees. This particular building also served as one of the company's six repair facilities and remained so for many years after the Hull Brook Street facility had closed. In addition to their High Street address, the company also traded at several other addresses in Stockton-on-Tees.*

125 *This 1909 postcard depicts a bemused crowd of onlookers as the cameraman takes his picture of Fore Street, Bridgwater. Lennards opened a branch at 13 Fore Street around 1906 and remained there until the early 1970s. Whilst the usual practice of trading under the parent company of The Public Benefit Boot Company prevailed right across the region, there were odd instances where Lennards opened under their own name, as in Bridgwater. Olivers, depicted in the background, are listed as trading at 17-18 Cornhill – a street that runs into Fore Street in central Bridgwater, so it is very likely that Lennards' premises were close by.*

126 *Around 1908 the company occupied premises on the right-hand side of this view of Gold Street, Northampton. They continued at that address until 1956 when they moved to 14 Abington Street where they traded until 1973 as Benefit Footwear.*

On February 5th 1908, the amount then appearing in the Balance Sheet representing goodwill (£12,000) was extinguished by accumulated reserve fund, confirmed Feb. 2nd 1909.

The Freehold Headquarters of the Company, situated in Queens Road, Bristol, (subject to a perpetual fee farm Rent of £300 per annum) were built by the Company for its own use, and the amount at which they stand in the Balance Sheet is less than cost. They are admittedly one of the finest blocks of buildings in Bristol, having a total area of 2,730 square yards, and a floor space of 75, 000 superficial feet, fitted with two electric lifts, fireproof floors, and the Courtyard arranged specially for dealing with and transporting goods. The buildings have

an extensive frontage to a most important thoroughfare, which is practically the gateway to the largest and most important residential neighbourhood in the West of England. Elevations are shown herewith, and the buildings are too well known to need further description. The shops on the ground floor are let on leases to responsible tenants at a total rental of upwards of £1,400 per annum. The adjoining Building Site (part of the Property belonging to the Company), has a total area of 2,270 square yards, and has just been let on lease for the purpose of a Skating Rink …

127 *Lennards had a number of branches in Kent including one situated on Cheriton Road, Folkestone.*

128 *Postcard of Carlton Street, Castleford, in the early 1900s. The Public Benefit Boot Company premises are on the extreme right with a canopy over the footpath. The firm made their mark in this Yorkshire mining town in the 1890s when Carlton Street had become a busy thoroughfare. This building was undoubtedly one of the many new buildings erected at the time and the firm moved into it around 1896 – remaining there until 1917. The company then, as in other towns, evaluated their trade and found the branch too large for their needs. They relocated to smaller premises at number 63 – further up and across the street. The branch manager for over twenty years was William North Driver, a man of considerable influence in the area – he helped to establish the nearby grand Free Library.*

129 *Logo used in Public Benefit Boot Company advertisements in 1909.*

130 *Close to Hull, in the busy town of Beverley, the Public Benefit Boot Company opened for business in Toll Gavel in the 1880s. This 1905 scene shows Toll Gavel looking towards Butcher Row. The street was an important trading thoroughfare and the company continued trading there under the Benefit Footwear name until the 1960s. Stead and Simpson, on the right, was a rival and similar in standing to the Public Benefit Boot Company. Stead and Simpson were also establishing a national network and the business continues to thrive today as one of the few independent footwear retailers in the country.*

131 *The company traded on Carr Street, Ipswich, for some decades. In this view of Carr Street, the Lyceum is on the right and further down on the right a spherical pointed roof identifies the Public Benefit building which was on the corner of Little Colman Street.*

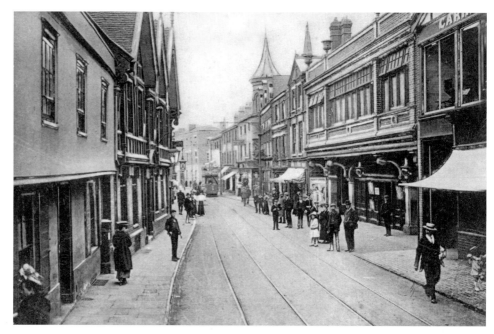

Lennards Limited have in the leases of their 130 retail branches (as per list herewith 123 open, 7 being fitted) a valuable property—not only has the goodwill of the business been entirely written off—but the fittings and fixtures have been depreciated 10% each year, so that as a going concern the fittings and fixtures are worth more than the amount at which they stand in the books of the Company.

During the twelve years since incorporation, Lennards Limited have never paid less than 7% on the Ordinary Shares. The business is conducted on a sound cash basis both for buying and selling, not a single penny is owing to trade creditors when the Balance Sheet is prepared at the end of each year.

An accountant's report in the same 1909 prospectus sets out the company's profit:

In accordance with your instructions we have examined the accounts of your Company for the past three years, and certify that the profits on the business, subject to Mortgage and Debenture Interest, were:

For the year ending 29th December, 1906
£13,753. 8. 8

Ditto ditto 28th December, 1907 £13,870.15. 9

Ditto ditto 2nd January, 1909 £16,241. 5. 6

These profits are arrived at after making full provision for Wear and Tear, Depreciation of Fixtures and Fittings, and Amortisation of Leasehold Properties, but without charging amounts appropriated to Reserve Account, or Depreciation of Freehold properties.

The Managing Director as Vendor to the Company is entitled under the Articles of Association to a proportion of net profits in excess of the amount required to provide 6% on Preference Shares and 10% on the Ordinary Shares …

132 *The Public Benefit Boot Company store on the corner of Lynn Street and Musgrave Street, Hartlepool in 1912. Opened in 1894, this was a typical branch in the North East where mining, shipbuilding and allied heavy industries dominated. The keenly priced rows of boots and shoes – the quality of which was beyond question – were targeted at the working classes.*

133 *The prominent Lennards Limited headquarters depicted in the 1920s.*

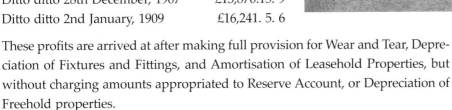

REGISTERED TRADE MARK

Lennards

FOR ❖ GOOD ❖ BOOTS ❖ AND ❖ SHOES.

At the bottom of the last page of the prospectus, immediately above the signature of the directors is the statement:

This Company is absolutely distinct from and has no connection with either the Public Benefit Boot Co., Ltd., Leeds, or Lennard Bros., Ltd., Leicester.

This statement suggests that there was no legal connection between these former partners, but the records indicate that a high degree of informal cooperation and

134 From around 1903 Public Benefit gained an important foothold in the city of Lincoln, firstly at 115 High Street where the company traded until about 1930. Another branch operated in Lincoln at 203 High Street from 1920 until the 1960s; this branch was next door to the Lloyds Bank building – the prominent building on the right with the cupola. Constructed for the Capital and Counties Bank between 1913 and 1919, Nikolaus Pevsner in 1964 referred to this significant building's design and in particular its cupola that has since been removed.

135 Public Benefit traded extensively in South Wales with over twenty branches in the Rhondda as well as in the large cities of Cardiff and Swansea. In Pontypridd the company traded from around 1900 at 6 Taff Street where their premises also opened on to Market Street. This view shows the junction of Taff Street (on the left) with Market Street on the right. The Public Benefit branch was located on the right side of Taff Street some distance past the tram. Signs for Olivers, another footwear dealer, can be seen on the left of Taff Street.

136 *The Public Benefit Boot Company traded on the south side of the Market Place, Peterborough, in the early 1900s and continued to have a presence for many decades. In this view, the company premises are on the right with the cathedral in the distance to the east.*

137 *In 1929 two stores were trading under the name of Lennards in Oswestry – one at Bailey Street and the other at 9 The Cross. Several rival boot stores are evident in this photograph of The Cross.*

138 *An interesting view of Chelmsford High Street where two Public Benefit shops opened around 1910. One was located at 37 High Street for a few years – on the right-hand side of the street close to Barnards Hotel. The other shop was at 87 High Street – this was on the left-hand side in the distance close to the classical Shire Hall building. This store operated under various names, including Lennards Ltd, until the 1970s.*

139 *During the 1920s and 1930s Lennards premises were a few doors down on the left of this view of High Street, Canterbury.*

agreement was maintained between the companies for over a quarter of a century.

Benefit Footwear produced a booklet in 1947 to celebrate 50 years of the company's history since the incorporation of 1897. The 32-page booklet 'Benefit Footwear Limited 1897–1947—a brief history', was well written but it gives scant reference and little importance to the role played by Lennards. The booklet clearly states that a gentlemen's agreement had existed since 1897 that neither company would open branches in the other company's area.

140 In Grimsby, Public Benefit occupied premises in Cleethorpes Road from 1882 until 1910 before they moved to Victoria Street. From the mid-1930s to the mid-1960s the company occupied premises at 110 Freeman Street in Grimsby. In this view of Freeman Street, the branch was situated on the left just a little further along from the Prince of Wales Theatre, the large building on the right. Frederick Franklin, a brother of William and George Franklin, managed the company's Grimsby branch for many years. Another brother, Samuel, owned considerable fishing and fish-marketing interests in Grimsby.

This appears slightly inaccurate as the two companies had cooperated with each other since 1897. They had opened branches in a variety of ways in a bid to help Lennard establish stores in the territories he had marked out as his own. An over riding objective was to beat any rivals in the region and this meant owner-ship of many branches was shared.

The company booklet mentions very little of the upheaval in the boardroom and resignation of the founder and directors—it appears to be a brief period in the history of the company that they would rather forget.

Public Benefit and Lennards worked tirelessly to become two separate com-panies. They continued to transfer assets and accelerated the process to reduce

141 Series of advertisements depicting various styles of footwear, published in the Hull News *in 1907.*

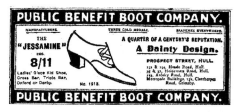

142 *Public Benefit opened premises at 47 Bradshawgate in Bolton around 1896 under the management of William Harker, son of Jabez Harker. From 1909 to the 1930s the company traded at 12-14 Bradshawgate where they were located when this photograph was taken in 1914.*

143 *This view of Lower High Street, Merthyr, shows everyone standing to one side waiting for something – possibly a tram – or was it the Public Benefit Boot Company's horse-drawn cart pulling the big boot? The company opened a shop about 1906 at 66 High Street in Merthyr and remained trading as Public Benefit until around 1916 when the name was changed to Lennards Limited.*

144 *In Wales an important branch in the 1920s through to at least the 1940s was situated at 175 Commercial Street in Newport. This branch was in the Westgate Buildings, the large building on the right in this photograph. The town hall in the distance has since been demolished.*

145 *This pre-First World War window display is typical with boots hanging outside or in the doorway, with large distinguishable price tags attached. The mirror seen in the doorway and partially concealed with shoeboxes was often used as a security device – reflecting the easily stolen footwear hanging on display. The location of this particular Public Benefit branch is unknown but there are indications that it was founded prior to 1897, possibly in Yorkshire or Derbyshire.*

146 *The Jessamine, Chatalaine, Cleopatra, Diplomat and Varsity were trademarks registered by the Public Benefit Boot Company in November and December 1905.*

147 *'Public Benefit for good boots and shoes' announces the sign above a shop on the right just past the tram. The company traded in various premises on King Street, South Shields, from 1899 until at least the 1940s. They occupied the branch depicted here at 79 King Street from 1899 until 1911 when they moved next door to 77 King Street until 1924. In the 1990s Shoefayre were operating from the King Street premises previously occupied by Public Benefit.*

148 *In the late 1890s the company traded at 10 Northgate in the West Yorkshire town of Halifax. Early in the century they moved to premises at 31 Crown Street, shown on the extreme right of the street.*

149 *Lennard Brothers had a major presence in Portsmouth and in the 1890s Commercial Road was one of the sites for a branch of their Mutual Boot Stores. This store reverted to trading as The Public Benefit Boot Company by 1897 and in later years Lennards Limited continued trading from various addresses along Commercial Road.*

the number of premises actually owned by Public Benefit. The transfer of stores in 1912 involved no fewer than 33 stores from Public Benefit based in Leeds to Lennards in Bristol. The same pattern continued in 1913 in an apparent attempt to balance carefully the numbers of stores held by each company. Throughout this entire period both companies still traded as The Public Benefit Boot Company Limited—another indicator of the continuing and extraordinary relationship between the two companies.

The 1913 Red Book of Commerce describes Lennards as 'leather, boot and shoe hosiery merchants with head office in Bristol and nearly 200 shops throughout England and Wales'. Further evidence exists that Lennards was still counting the branches owned by the Leeds company as their own. The Public Benefit financial accounts for that year indicate that they appeared also to be counting stores not wholly owned by them. It was 1914 before Public Benefit and Lennards finally severed their relationship more completely. This was signalled to the public by changing store fascias (that had formerly advertised Public Benefit Boot Company) to show the store name as simply Lennards Limited.

In March 1917 the Public Benefit business activities in Leeds were featured in a supplement in *The*

150 Like many of the Public Benefit premises, the branch in High Street, Exeter, was located close to a well-known landmark – in this case, the Guildhall. The branch at 211-212 High Street can be seen in this photograph immediately past the Guildhall. The company's distinctive horse-drawn boot trademark was displayed prominently on the side of the building. In the early years of the century the company also traded at 170 Sidwell Street and at 25 Goldsmith Street, Exeter.

151 In the early 1900s a branch was opened at Doggerbank House, Church Street, Malvern, not visible in this photograph. By 1914 Lennards had erected their sign on the fascia as part of continuing efforts to forge ahead with independence from Public Benefit.

152 Metal shoehorn engraved with the company name and trademark, probably given away to customers as a promotional item.

Shoe and Leather and Allied Trades News showing portraits of the directors and photographs of the Leeds headquarters and principal branches at Hull, Birmingham, Derby and Sheffield. The text proclaimed that 'The number of branches has now increased to 140 including six repairing factories'. The criteria for counting branches as their branches had obviously changed as a year or so earlier both companies were boasting over 200 branches each.

The 140 Public Benefit premises consisted of 111 branches, six repair facilities, six branches trading in Lennard territory but owned by Public Benefit, and 17 jointly-owned branches. The jointly-owned branches consisted of a branch in Fulham, four branches in Wales and 12 branches in the West Country.

153 For several decades early in the century, Public Benefit had a branch in Mostyn Street, depicted here, in the picturesque seaside town of Llandudno. The company premises were in the distance on the right.

154 Another branch was located at 33 Kings Road, Southsea in the early 1900s and from 1918 to at least 1940 it was trading from 57 Kings Road. This view is of busy Kings Road early in the century.

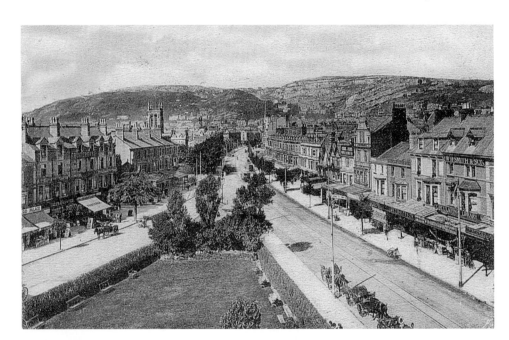

5 Testing Times

The First World War took a heavy toll on British business and Public Benefit and Lennards were not spared. There is stirring testament to that fact in the Lennards' report of February 1917 when the chairman, Thomas Lennard, read the following statement:

> This is our third war balance sheet, and I cannot speak too highly, firstly of the patriotism of the men of Lennards Ltd, and secondly of the whole staff who have worked together loyally under circumstances not only unprecedented; but under difficulties of transit, changes, restrictions, and shortage of labour, material and goods, that would be unbearable were we not convinced that the British empire is championing a sacred and just cause against a most unscrupulous foe, and that our final victory is certain.

> We have 200 men serving with the colours, 197 of whom were volunteers. The wages made good and the war bonus as wages paid by the company for the year amounts to over £4,000. Each Christmas we have sent a parcel to each soldier; most appreciative letters in acknowledgment have been received.

> During the year I sent our buyer, Mr. W. Dickson, to Canada and the United States, and I have to compliment him upon his devotion to duty.

> Owing to the shortage of labour, we have closed three repairing factories and we are closing eleven branches. We consider our trade, after being exceptionally

155 Postcard of the Peace Day parade 19 July 1919 passing by the company premises in Uttoxeter. The shop appears to be closed for the day as on these occasions a holiday would often be declared.

156 *This view shows the company premises at 33 Boothferry Road, Goole, a site the company occupied from 1896 for at least three decades. This branch used their exterior wall to full advantage for advertising 'Boots-Benefit-Shoes'– it could easily be seen from the passing trains and traffic.*

157 *In 1869 Goole's second railway station was built on Boothferry Road and several private buildings were erected between there and the original town. The centre of Goole moved into Boothferry Road and from the 1880s rapid development took place on both sides of the railway line. In this view the Public Benefit branch was about halfway down on the right side of the road.*

158 *This was the second Public Benefit branch to open at Goole – operating at 19 Bridge Street from 1904 until at least 1917 and possibly the 1920s. The fascia style suggests that the photograph was taken in the 1920s when the company was refurbishing a number of branches. A boom in manufacturing followed the First World War and this may have inspired the company to upgrade their image – in this case giving more emphasis to the word 'Benefit'.*

159 *A promotional postcard produced by Lennards Ltd under the Public Benefit Boot Company name.*

useful to the government, has had to put up with more difficulties than others—in the commandeering of our material at cost price, instead of at market price; the unnecessary anxiety, trouble and expense caused by the War Council Order cancelling agreements made with the military authorities as to labour, referring all individual cases to local tribunals, some of whom have referred them back again. In normal times we would not submit to such treatment, but now we assent to any sacrifice to support a really national government, to the end that we obtain a victorious peace.

The report goes on to cover the profit margin for 1916 and other normal company concerns such as the opening of new branches and the reduction in value of fixtures and fittings. The next statement is also interesting and gives an account of what was happening during those times of crisis and the contribution many companies made to the war effort:

160 *Repair docket for £3 7s. 9d. dated 1 January 1919. Terms were strictly cash.*

161 *Public Benefit operated two premises in Whitley Bay during the 1920s – one at 40 The Esplanade and the other at 215 Whitley Road. By the 1930s the Esplanade store had closed but the Whitley Road premises remained until the 1960s. This view shows Whitley Road as it appeared early in the century.*

I do not think there is any other item upon which I need comment until we come to the distribution of the profit, but with regard to the reserve of £10,000 for excess profit duty we are bearing an exceptional burden; to select any one year and say that 60 per cent of any profit in excess of the profit earned that year shall belong to the state, whether the result be due to war profits or not, is unjust;

162 In the early 1900s William Harker traded as a boot and shoe retailer at 42 Northgate Street in the ancient town of Chester. Around 1907, and for the following few decades, the business traded at the same address under the Public Benefit name.

163 For more than forty years The Public Benefit Boot Company had premises at 86 Eastgate in Louth. This branch was on the left of this view of Eastgate.

164 The Public Benefit Boot Company traded at 4 Market Place in Driffield from around 1913 until at least 1937. In this view of Market Place the premises were some distance down on the right, close to the corner of George Street.

if we pay it willingly now, it is with the hope that the first revision for peace taxation will remove or revise this tax.

The Public Benefit annual report of 1916 offers a similar but shorter version of the wartime difficulties:

The demands of the war brought with it many new and unforseen difficulties—labour, supplies, transport and stocks—but all are being handled with care and forethought. Over 83% of the staff is now serving the country, and the directors have made provision for the wives of the married men, and are proud of the fact that three of their employees, corporal Geo. Dickinson (a nephew of the managing director), Sergt. P. Earl and Private H. Beresford—have gained the military medal for brave conduct in the field, but regret the loss of several valued servants who have made the sacrifice.

Under the able chairmanship of Mr John Kirby and the careful, capable management of Mr Brow Dickinson JP, the returns and profits have steadily increased year by year.

After the Great War there was a mini-boom as the country's war machine was dismantled and people demanded an end to the prolonged shortages of the past few years. For a time at least, people would have jobs as the work of rebuilding the country proceeded. Manufacturing of all kinds was stepped up to meet the strong demand for a multitude of goods. Footwear manufacturers swung heavily back into production and it wasn't long before supply outstripped demand to the point of causing a slump in prices. This was a costly experience for everyone, as retail stock had to be written down.

February 1919 saw the two Lennard Brothers directors, Samuel Briers and Disney Barlow, sail from Liverpool aboard the *Lapland* for New York.

165 *Postcard view around 1903 looking down Prospect Street, Hull. The Public Benefit Boot Company premises are on the right.*

166 *Built in 1920, the Liberty Shoe factory stood on Eastern Boulevard, Leicester, until its demolition in 2003. It was a notable example of reinforced concrete construction. The famous landmark from the top of the building stood in an adjacent football ground for some years until it was placed in storage pending a decision about its future.*

167 *The Liberty trademark registered in August 1901 by Lennard Brothers Limited of 85 Asylum Street, Leicester. The registration covered boots, shoes, slippers and other footwear.*

They spent several weeks in America and top of their list was meeting with colleagues at the United Shoe Manufacturing Company of New York where no doubt they exchanged ideas about the latest footwear manufacturing techniques. For almost two decades Lennard Brothers had been very successfully marketing their popular *Liberty* brand of footwear – the brand mark featured the Statue of Liberty in an ellipse with the inscription *Liberty & Freedom*. It seems that the

directors were very enthusiastic to see the real Statue of Liberty in New York harbour and it was not long after they returned to England that a replica Statue of Liberty proudly appeared on top of their newly built factory on Eastern Boulevard, Leicester. Designed by H.H. Thompson, the building was widely regarded as a notable early example of reinforced concrete construction. The company name of Lennard Brothers was subsequently changed to Liberty Shoes and the building became known as Liberty Building. The landmark statue stared blankly out over the river for seventy years but when the building eventually fell

168 Public Benefit opened in Sunderland around 1899 on High Street. The company sign is on the right at 260-261 High Street where this branch traded from 1915 until 1935. Sunderland was always an important trading base for the company and around 1902 they opened an additional branch on Hendon Road. In the early 1920s another branch was opened at 75 Hylton Road and remained there until the 1960s when it was taken over by the British Shoe Corporation.

169 A misty winter mood is captured in this 1920s photograph of Derby people on the corner of St Peter's Street and Babington Lane with the Public Benefit premises on the right.

170 In 1905 the company established a branch in East Street, Chichester, and traded for the first decade under the Public Benefit name, then as Lennards Limited. The large premises of Lennards were centrally located adjacent to the Market Cross in the 1920s, consistent with the company's long-held policy of securing striking locations close to significant landmarks.

into disrepair the statue was moved to the Main Stand at the adjacent Filbert Street Football Ground. Her hundredweight torch, which tumbled to the pavement during a severe frost attack, has been faithfully restored.

In this era many Public Benefit stores in the North East were sited in mining villages and towns. These premises were small and conveniently close to the pit head—the miners would pass the store on their way to work. More often than not the Public Benefit shop would be the only shop selling footwear to the mining community and therefore the company enjoyed a monopoly. The Public Benefit store was seen by the community as the obvious place to buy their footwear.

The company's success in these mining communities was in part due to the fact that they were often the only footwear shop in the area but there were

also other factors. Due to the severe post-war world depression, stores necessarily moved away from a cash only basis and into credit arrangements—a system of club or credit cheques became customary. These were arrangements commonly made with money-lenders who would issue a cheque or club to spend at the store and the money would be repaid to the lender over a period of time.

A deep trust developed between the branches and their customers and this is evident in the common practice of allowing customers to take home footwear on approval. The trust that developed in turn earned the branch a good reputation.

Former employees have passed on interesting glimpses of life in the Public Benefit shops of the 1920s, particularly from the North East mining towns. The Blyth branch in Regent Street was a store that was well remembered. The highly regarded store manager, Mr Frear, cycled to work each day without fail. He was seen as a pleasant man and he allowed customers to take home two or three pairs of shoes or boots for a family member to try on. Possibly the family bread-winner was a miner with little time to visit the shop, so he would be able to try on footwear at home.

171 The company had numerous branches in the London region including one at 294 Regent Street in the 1920s, situated at the Portland Place end of Regent Street. This view of the street at the time suggests a slower pace and a more peaceful time.

172 Benefit Footwear staff from the entire North Eastern region on a company outing to Whitley Bay in the 1930s. The group included employees from Blyth, Newcastle and many of the mining communities such as Easington Colliery. In an age when holidays were fewer than today, annual company outings were popular and show the high degree of comradeship amongst the company staff.

Despite the vicious worldwide depression of the 1920s the company held its position reasonably well. A few uneconomical branches were closed, others were refurbished and even a few new branches were opened. New suppliers also brought differing styles of footwear and this resulted in fresh impetus and a push into new avenues of business.

The company board changed hands in 1929 after an offer was accepted from J.F. Marrian of Worcester and his associates. This latest development brought with it not only changes to the board room, but a major reorganisation of many aspects of the company.

Competition in the footwear trade was fierce and had grown steadily from the end of the First World War. A plan was implemented to meet this threat—the first stage being a huge sale of old stock that had been greatly reduced in price. The gigantic sale was a phenomenal success in branches across the country. With most of the old stock cleared from the stores in the sale, new suppliers submitted more modern footwear designs and Public Benefit had given itself a much better chance of succeeding in the new, more competitive environment.

One significant aspect of the reorganisation introduced by J.F. Marrian and his associates was a shift in emphasis from self-manufacturing of footwear to a gradual buying in of stock. The demand for heavy work boots had diminished so rather than spend money on adapting the factory to produce the newer lighter styles of footwear it was more viable to buy in, especially as good manufacturers and suppliers were in abundance. This major change led in 1934 to the end of 30 years of footwear manufacturing at the company's headquarters at St Paul's House in Leeds. The change to buying in meant that good suppliers were able to furnish the company with a wide range of the latest products and this in turn significantly changed the ethos of the company.

It was also around this period that ladies' fashions were beginning to impact dramatically on the footwear industry. Along with their rivals, both Public Benefit and Lennards sought to capture a good share of this emerging market. An extensive programme of refurbishment and shop fitting was implemented during the early 1930s and continued right up to the onset of the Second World War. Most of the existing

173 To meet the demands from their expanding business, Lennards increased their manufacturing capacity substantially in 1930 when they acquired a third factory in Northamptonshire.

175 *Colonel Ernest Lennard, Managing Director of Lennards Limited in 1931.*

176 *The entrance hall and main staircase in the Lennards Building, Bristol, in the 1930s.*

branches were transformed to place emphasis on the growing ladies' fashion trade. Some shops were closed, perhaps too costly to transform, but at this time Public Benefit refurbished around 190 branches. This must have been very difficult in the light of reduced consumer spending and widespread unemployment at the time.

In the 1920s and 1930s Lennards Limited had major operations in Bristol, London, Leicester and Northampton. In 1922 another Lennard family member, Colonel Ernest Lennard, joined the board and later became Managing Director. Between 1929 and 1931 the company's retail outlets grew quickly from 200 to 250 branches. They also vigorously and successfully expanded their mail order business. Lennards' comprehensive catalogues of the time contained brief extracts from the numerous letters of appreciation received from over 80 different lands and colonies. The quotes from correspondence gave an idea of the considerable market penetration of the Lennards mail order business. As well as appreciative remarks from England, Scotland, Ireland and Wales,

Genuine **KANGAROO** Australian **HIDE**

BOOTS AND SHOES

A NEW departure in men's footwear. Genuine Australian Kangaroo Hides make excellent leather, which is supple as Glacé Kid, but much tougher and stronger. The tanning process produces a highly polished surface that will not crack or peel and these models are recommended for hard wear. The grain markings are similar to Glacé Kid and this innovation provides really distinctive footwear at popular prices.

STYLE 9131
14/9

For suitable Hosiery see page 47

STYLE 9131
Black Kangaroo Hide is used for this neat Oxford pattern shoe, with selected leather sole, attached on the hand-sewn principle. Light in weight and durable.

Also in rich Brown shade of Kangaroo Hide, quote style 9130.

STYLE 9133
Lace boot cut from rich Brown Kangaroo Hide. A welted model that is neat, light in weight, and thoroughly reliable in every way.

Also in Black, quote style 9132.

New productions by Lennards

STYLE 9133
16/9

The most wear for the least expenditure

BRITAIN'S BEST BOOTMAKERS
Lennards
BRISTOL. NORTHAMPTON. LONDON. LEICESTER
AND 250 BRANCHES

177 *Innovations featured in the 1931 Lennards' catalogue include men's footwear made from genuine Australian kangaroo hide – said to make excellent leather.*

178 *The cover of Lennards' 1931 catalogue that contained 168 pages of merchandise.*

179 *Shoes from Lennards, 1931 mail order catalogue.*

STYLE 311
12/9

STYLE 5331

STYLE 303
10/9

comments were printed from far-flung countries including Uganda, Jamaica, Ceylon, Egypt, Siam, USA, Borneo, India, Norway, Panama, Australia, Canada, Burma, Persia, Turkey, Holland, Greece and many more.

These customers' comments in the 1931 catalogue suggested, of course, that they were very well satisfied:

Sarawak: 'Shoes fitted well and are very neat and well-finished and are the kind of footwear everyone should wear.'

Jamaica: 'The low price of your footwear is impossible to believe.'

Nigeria: 'Cannot explain how glad I am to have received the shoes to my entire satisfaction.'

New Zealand: 'Despite the Duty, goods met with much approval and further orders will follow.'

Gold Coast: 'Your world-famed boots and shoes are beyond comparison, but not beyond the reach of all pockets.'

Bermuda: 'Footwear, also goods from your General Service Department, are quite satisfactory.'

India: 'Pleased with fitting, also the attention and prompt execution you give.'

Panama: 'Your footwear has no rival in this country.'

Australia: 'Shoes to hand and am well pleased.'

China: 'All satisfactory and a good fit.'

Syria: 'Your footwear is superior in quality and wear to all others I have tried.'

Lennards' profusely illustrated catalogue offered the gentleman Oxford shoes (8s. 9d.); Derby shoes (10s. 9d.); patent leather shoes with crocodile grain insertions (12s. 9d.); lace boots (16s. 9d.); sharkskin shoes (30d.); Brown Lizard skin shoes (42 d.); Brogue shoes (18s. 6d.); Officer's service boots (30s.); football boots (6s. 11d.); Cheltenham riding boots (42s.); polo or hunting boot (63s.) and tennis shoes (1s. 11d.);

The ladies were tempted with such things as calf shoes (10s.9d.); box Derby boots (11s. 6d.); Derbyette shoes (12s. 9d.); Eastbourne sandal shoes (8s. 11d.);

LENNARDS PLAYING CARDS

Produced by a well-known British House. Lennards' Registered mark on back printed in photogravure. Thousands of packs sold at this price (actual cost of production), and both at home ar there is demand Best ivory

(*Weight 6-ozs.*)

No. S975 1/-

180 According to the 1931 advertisement there was 'enormous demand' for Lennards' best ivory finish playing cards with thousands of packs sold for the price of one shilling – the actual cost of production. The playing cards came neatly boxed, and printed in red on the back of each was the registered mark 'Lennards World-Famed Boots & Shoes'.

181 The British Postal Authorities established a Post Office within the Lennards' business premises to facilitate the large amount of mail-order sales they were generating. Overseas parcels were driven a short distance to the Bristol docks.

182 *Gentlemen in tropical far-off places could feel well dressed if they had access to a Lennards Limited catalogue.*

183 *In their annual catalogues Lennards Limited listed their many branch addresses. In 1931 they referred to 250 branch establishments.*

brocade evening shoes (6s. 11d.); black satin evening shoes (12s. 9d.); rubber Wellington boots (6s. 11d.) and rubber soled plimsolls (1s. 11d.).

There were an increasing number of requests for Lennards to purchase other good to be shipped to their overseas customers along with footwear that was ordered. In response to this demand, Lennards established a general service section as part of their mail order organisation and in 1927 they bought the business and stock of a Bristol mail order specialist Wentworths.

In the 1931 catalogue of 168 pages, two-thirds of the pages were devoted to footwear and the remaining pages carried details of other items that could be ordered through Lennards General Service Department. Each of these articles, like Lennards footwear, was guaranteed as 'British-made and produced by British labour, British capital and British brains'.

The catalogue offer included shirts, linen collars, pyjamas, underwear, artistic neckwear, hats, British woollies and scarves, tea sets, attaché cases, alarm clocks,

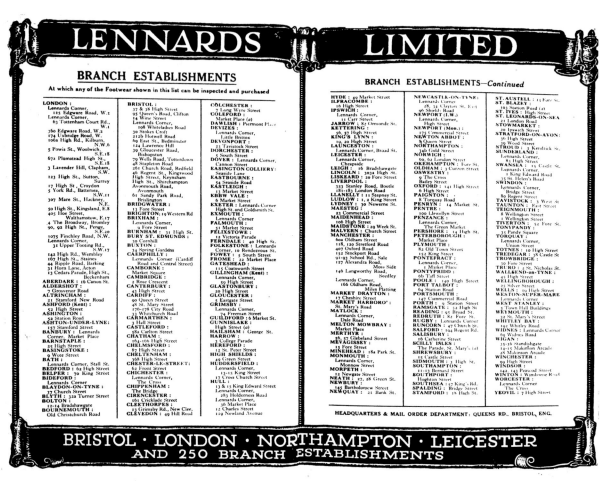

stoves, fountain pens, razors, box cameras, soldering sets, pipes and cigarette cases, books, umbrellas, musical instruments, handbags, screwdrivers, torches, cutlery, tropical remedies, watches and jewellery.

The discerning customer in the colonies could make life infinitely more bearable and refined by ordering an illustrated note book on the prevention of malaria (6d.); a hammock (8s.6d.); a 22-ct gold wedding ring (17s.6d.); Lennards' own brand of playing cards (1s.); dumb-bell muscle developers (10s.6d.); a beetle trap – known to catch thousands in one night (2s.); a portable gramophone (£2 12s.6d.); a full-sized rosewood piccolo (4s.6d.) or a 6ft British bunting flag ready for hoisting (10s.6d.).

Colonial gentlemen could order a briar pipe (2s.6d.); an all-wool bathing costume (7s.11d.); a book entitled 'Complete letter writer for gentlemen' (1s.2d.); a bow tie (1s.) a pith helmet (15s.6d.); a straw boater hat (5s.); a tweed cap (2s.6d.); or if he wanted to look even more resplendent he could choose an ebonised walking stick with a two-inch silver knob (6s.6d.) and a collapsible top hat (21s.).

Lennards maintained a staff of experienced and highly trained orthopaedic experts and catalogue customers suffering from foot ailments were requested to write to the company's Mr William George for free advice as to treatment and exercises.

For distant mail order customers who couldn't find items they required in the catalogue, Lennards operated a service for providing advice and obtaining a wide range of British merchandise:

A friend in England

When you need friendly service in England that only someone on the spot can give you – advice and suggestions about shops, materials or personal requirements, or when you need goods not illustrated in this catalogue, write to Miss Enid Croft or to Mr Dennis Barlow, c/o Lennards, Bristol, England.

These members of our staff are detailed to assist distant customers in every way possible and they will willingly carry out any enquiry or shopping commission for you as they would for a personal friend. This is part of our service and there is of course no charge other than the net purchase price of anything bought for

184 Lennards famous 'Trek' boot was designed for 'army officers, gentlemen farmers, sportsmen and travellers in many lands'.

185 Glamorous evening shoes from Lennards' 1931 catalogue.

you. Such purchases made always at the best possible sources and at the very keenest prices on your behalf.

Both Miss Croft and Mr Barlow are experienced shoppers, each has an assistant available in London and each may be written to with assurance of painstaking regard to your wishes, however intimate or confidential.

Another of the many changes taking place during the 1920s and 1930s was the title on the Public Benefit Boot Company shop fascias. Abbreviated to read BENEFIT, the simplified title could be presented much larger and bolder on the store fascias. The official full company title remained, however, and was used on stationery and official company documents, etc.

Negotiations commenced in 1937 for the purchase of 50 retail shoe stores belonging to the Amies Wallace group operating in the Midlands and London areas. Some of those conflicted with existing Benefit shops and were closed immediately but the bulk of the premises, around forty, were kept and re-fitted as Benefit shops.

Following the extensive modernisation of the branches and the successful use of the word 'Benefit' on the shop fascias, it was deemed appropriate to change formally the company title to Benefit Footwear Limited. This was decided in 1939 but, because of the outbreak of war, the company was not officially registered under this title until 20 March 1946. The original title, Public Benefit

186 A simpler but no less effective enamel advertising plate.

187 Apprentices undergoing examination at the Brook Street repair facility, Hull, in the late 1930s. The photo is probably of a City and Guilds Practical Exam. The only Benefit employee is in the white coat overall and the other individuals would be employees of other companies. The qualified overseer acting as examiner was likely a repair manager of James Coombes and Company, identified by the distinctive brown smock peculiar to that company in those days.

188 Around 1910 Lennards opened a branch in the quaint market town of Devizes. They traded at 8 Little Brittox and continued to establish yet another of the famed 'Lennards Corner' branches. A rival store, Stead and Simpson, is on the left of this view of The Brittox.

189 A horse and cart stand outside the large arched window of the building occupied during the 1930s by Public Benefit at 23 King Edward Street, Hull. Other boot retailers operated on this part of the street including Tylers (immediately behind the tram) and Abbot Bros (on the far right of the picture). The large monument was erected as a tribute to the Hull MP, William Wilberforce — remembered for his important contribution to anti-slavery reforms.

Boot Company, which was conceived by the founder William Franklin around 70 years earlier—had stood the test of time very well but had become 'a little unwieldy for modern times'.

A former Public Benefit employee, Mrs Johnson of Blyth, gives some interesting insight into working at the Blyth branch in the 1930s. She worked firstly as a junior girl on a wage of 50 pence per week before progressing to become a first sales assistant. On the occasions when Mr Frear the manager was absent, Mrs Johnson managed the store and her wages were increased to £2.50. Work hours were long, from 9.00 a.m. to 7.00 p.m. or often later. Staff had Wednesday afternoons off. Mrs Johnson recalls working one particular Christmas Eve when at the stroke of midnight, a customer, having noticed staff were still working, insisted on spending her 'club' on a pair of shoes. Although the Blyth shop had carpets, stools and mirrors there was no heating and

staff and customers alike shivered in the winter. Managers and inspectors always insisted on keeping the door wide open to encourage custom. However Mrs Johnson ignored the ruling whenever she was placed in charge by closing the door and she found that potential customers would simply try the door handle and walk in. Children, particularly boys with thin legs, would try on hob nail

190 Public Benefit traded initially from the 1890s at Foregate in Worcester and subsequently moved to large prominent premises depicted on the left of this view of The Cross. The Lennards' name appears in the window displays and there is a large Public Benefit sign across the top of this huge centrally located building.

191 In 1900 Public Benefit had two branches in the old naval base of Plymouth – one at 82 Old Town Street and the other at 9 Union Street. Over the years the company traded at several other addresses on Old Town Street and Union Street. This postcard view shows Union Street in the 1920s.

boots and would be bought boots that were always two sizes too large to allow for growth—the same rule applied for the girls.

A lady from another pit town, Ashington, described the type of boots and shoes worn by some miners:

> We used to stock a green pigskin boot and shoes, my father was a miner but he always wore the shoe. I believe the price was either 8/11 or 10/6 (between 45

to 52 pence). I remember the prevalent smell of leather and Wellingtons, and I would rub Dubbin into the leather boots to keep them supple. Large boots hung up in the Benefit shops were commonplace as a trademark, but sadly few have survived some even thrown out when BSC took over. We used to have a great big boot in the shop and we told the children it was a giant's boot but unfortunately it was thrown out when Freeman, Hardy and Willis took over the shop and they did a refit.

193 In Grimsby the company traded in the important shopping thoroughfare of Victoria Street from 1910 until 1935.

Mrs E. Hunter of Bedlington in Northumberland described the shop there as being small and sited approximately three hundred yards from the pithead and also close to the market place. She described a shoe available there called a 'Rinker'.

They were black, patent leather bottoms with mauve coloured suede tops, with little hooks on each side which we crossed over with lace and tied at the top. The Bedlington branch opened six days per week from 9:00 am until around 6:00 pm but remained open until 8:00 pm on a Saturday evening.

Another former Benefit Footwear employee, Olive Smeatham, began working for the company in 1934 at the Whitley Bay branch. She confirmed that

194 The company traded from at least the early 1900s in the well-known university town of Oxford – firstly at 39 Queen Street from around 1907 and later at several addresses on High Street. Lennards' premises are seen on the extreme left of this view looking down High Street, Oxford.

the company was selling its own brand of footwear at various prices depending on quality:

> Prices for men's footwear ranged from 10/6 to one guinea with a free bone shoehorn included. The ladies' shoes started at 6/11 and ranged up to 14/11. Ladies' stocking available in Hose at 1/-, Lisle silk though sold at 1/11 because they were a heavy quarter-inch-thick wool type. Assistants were expected to make extra sales on items such as shoe creams and boot polish with all pairs of shoes sold. Customers considered wearability more important than looks—they wanted stylish footwear but they wanted it to be good quality, well-produced and strong.

The Whitley Bay branch, according to Olive Smeatham, was a moderately sized shop with around ten to twelve heavy chairs and well-cushioned seats at each side of a screen. Gents were seated on one side of the room, ladies and children on the other. Floor coverings were basic and consisted of linoleum with a strip of carpet that had to be kept clean by the female staff. Uniforms were expected to be dresses of a mid-blue shade provided by staff themselves with no reimbursement or uniform allowance from the company.

Part of the success of the Benefit Footwear stores stemmed from the fact that they continued to cater to local demand. For instance, the branch in the seaside town of Whitley Bay sold large quantities of rubber bathing shoes and sandshoes which city shops would call plimsolls. At the Whitley Bay shop, only one pair of each type of footwear would be kept on display and the bulk of the stock

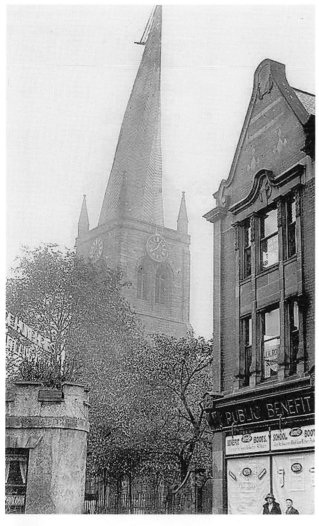

195 In the Derbyshire town of Chesterfield, Public Benefit were initially at 6 Corporation Street from the mid-1890s. Around 1910 they moved to a newly built building at 21 Stephenson Place where they stayed for at least the following three decades. The Stephenson Place premises depicted here were adjacent to the Rutland Arms public house and Chesterfield's famous crooked spire.

196 Leeds Headrow branch opened in 1931 sporting the strong 'Benefit' image on the prominent Thornton Buildings. During the 1950s the store traded late on Saturday evenings and would often be visited by Public Benefit's Managing Director Tom Eggleton. The story is told of how Eggleton and his wife, on the way to the theatre in their Lagonda car, would stop to check on business. The building still maintains a commanding position in the Headrow shopping precinct.

197 The picturesque Derbyshire spa town of Buxton where the Public Benefit could be found at 43 Spring Gardens in the 1930s. This photograph depicts Spring Gardens on a sunny day with shadows from the trees stretching across the road and people generally relaxing – on the grass, in chairs – with no motor vehicles to spoil the tranquillity.

198 *In the coal-mining regions houses and shops were usually built around the collieries and Public Benefit saw these communities as fertile ground to open branches. The company established a branch in Seaside Lane at Easington Colliery in Durham around 1914 and remained there for several decades. In this view, miners' houses are seen adjacent to the colliery.*

199 *In this 1930-1940 era view of Seaside Lane, ladies chat outside the Public Benefit premises – the third shop from the left. These mining communities were close knit and they worked and played hard. Community recreation included the village football and cricket teams, whippet racing, pit pony racing and the colliery's brass band. The local pubs and carnivals also provided opportunities to relax which was important for the miners who constantly faced the hardship and dangers of working in the pit. Tragedy struck this village in 1951 when a pit disaster occurred.*

was stored down in the cellar—the staff negotiated wooden steps and used a handrail made from hard, rough twine to access the stock. It is not too difficult to imagine the poor staff running up and down those steps, slipping, falling and running into each other to retrieve the slippers, Wellingtons, summer goods and surplus stock.

Wages were low but improved over time with selling techniques, incentives and commission on sales. Older stock and discontinued lines were pushed in earnest as the assistant could expect to earn a *spiff* (one penny in the pound extra) and sometimes this incentive was extended to a whole shilling for selling faded or soiled goods. Sales assistants of the time were expected to know the names of the bones in the feet and to measure children's feet correctly to achieve a good fit.

6 A New Era Unfolds

The commencement of the Second World War brought new and terrible dangers to civilian populations throughout England. The threat of aerial bombardment had existed previously with the Zeppelin but the German Luftwaffe was far more destructive. During the blitz, the St Paul's Street headquarters was deemed to be in considerable danger. As the building contained huge quantities of footwear it was decided to transfer all stock to three warehouses at Guiseley, 10 miles from the centre of Leeds. For the duration of the war the Royal Pay Corps occupied the company headquarters in St Paul's Street. The very successful branches at Prospect Street, Hull and Smithford Street, Coventry, were both damaged beyond repair and were later demolished. Many of the company premises experienced near misses including the St Paul's Street headquarters.

Former employee Bill Clayton told of his experiences during the onset of war. A mine fell in the station yard at Blyth as Bill, then aged 17, was on Fire watch. The window of the Benefit Footwear shop was blown out, sending shoes into the main street—leaving Bill frantically gathering up the shoes as quickly as possible.

With so many people involved in the war effort, shortages of staff once again caused concern and it was to the great armies of women that the country turned. They replaced men on the land, in factories, offices, hospitals and shops—proving

200 *The ruined shell of the Public Benefit store on Prospect Street, Hull, after an air raid in May 1941. The premises were eventually replaced by a modern addition to Hull Central Library.*

201 *The Scarborough shopfront was typical of many stores that were refurbished before the Second World War.*

themselves to be extremely capable regardless of the role they undertook.

When the war ended, a vast army of demobilised men returned to their old jobs. However, one young woman of the time, Olive Smeatham, found gainful employment travelling from Benefit branch to branch training the men in the changes that had taken place during their long absences. She then became a window dresser and continued to work for the company for many years.

Mrs A. Wilson, another wartime employee, recalls that large numbers of handicapped workers were employed at the repair factory in Templar Street, Leeds. Mrs Wilson's first job was putting socks in shoes for 25 shillings per week but she progressed to become a stitcher for an extra five shillings per week. Her wartime memories remain vivid: 'During the war the boss, Harry Edgar Wright, got the contract to mend army boots and we had lorry loads of soldiers pulling up outside the factory. They sat outside whilst their boots were mended as they waited'.

Mr Fred Lunn, who worked at the Templar Street repair factory, recalls an amusing incident that tells something of the frugal wartime years: 'I worked on raw heels and we received this pair of shoes from Harewood House. It had the royal insignia from HRH the Duchess of Harewood. The note read 'Will you please reheel this pair of shoes and send back the old heels as they might fit another pair of shoes'. Mr Lunn believes the manager kept the letter as a keepsake.

Bill Clayton recalls that shortly after the war shoes were in short supply until full production could be reinstated and all stock would arrive by van from Leeds on a Thursday morning. The local women learned of this and would form long queues waiting for 'nylons' and the new fashion shoes. 'We would only get a couple of boxes of Kaiser Bondor [the brand name] so we had to try and make sure the same people didn't get them every week.' Most shops had to resort to locking doors whilst unpacking occurred to stop the shop from being overrun with excited customers.

202 This view of the branch at 22 Onslow Street, Guildford, was taken sometime in the 1960s. The building was demolished in the early 1970s as part of the Friary shopping centre development.

203 Shoe repairs price list issued November 1940 showing price increases due to the extra cost of materials and labour. The company is noted on the price list as 'R.A.F. & Army Boot Repairs Contractors'.

Arthur Hudson, who managed the Benefit repair facility in Templar Street, Leeds, remembers another legend from this period. Both Arthur Hudson and Fred Lunn recall Bill the Benefit Boot Man and provided graphic details of this well-known character. Bill would walk around the centre of Leeds with a large Benefit boot around his neck. He befriended another down-and-out character called Woodbine Liz and both would stand outside Leeds Market. The big boot had no heel and it fitted over Bill's head and the laces tied around his neck. Whenever he took it off to go to the toilet, kids would sit in the boot. He conducted his rounds until approximately 1950 and his route took in Templar Street to the bus station, around the market, Corn Exchange, Boar Lane, up Briggate to the old dispensary and back to Templar Street. His ports of call included The Commercial Club, *The Robin Hood*, *The Golden Cock*, The Central Market and *The Whip*. The manager at the time, Mr Wright, would send apprentices out to check up on Bill the Benefit Boot Man from time to time.

A large fire in the Templar Street repair factory provided some excitement in the final hours of 1964. Arthur Hudson recalls it was a dramatic event:

I can be quite precise about the time and date of the fire at the Leeds, Templar Street, Central Repair Factory; it was discovered at 5.00am Thursday 31st December 1964, at which time I was called from my home being the number one key holder of the premises. By the time I arrived at the scene shortly after, the firemen had already broken down the main entrance doors. The fire started in the Chinese restaurant situated above the factory. The Min Sin Chinese Restaurant to give it its full title was completely gutted, everything in the factory below was completely flooded and therefore rendered totally inoperable. I recall sitting in the car of the police superintendent during the height of the blaze and complaining to him about the antics of the firemen who appeared to be throwing bags of potatoes down the staircase leading up to the restaurant, instead of making greater effort to save my factory, it was only when the 'bags of potatoes' got up and started

204 One of a series of postcards celebrating life in London between the wars – this one delightfully capturing a quiet moment spent having one's boots polished.

running away did we realise that they were Chinese members of staff who were 'illegally' living in the storeroom of the restaurant and had been refusing to evacuate the place.

The total number of staff employed at the factory at that time was 150, and in order to avoid any loss of jobs, I had them transported daily to work in our other establishments, situated at Bradford (Saxone), Doncaster (Saxone), Huddersfield (Trueform) and the new Benefit factory that we had opened at 33 Queen Victoria Street, Leeds some six months previous. We eventually opened another factory at the bottom end of Templar Street some nine months later. That factory became subject of a local authority, compulsory purchase order some 18 months later, at which time we opened a factory in Roundhay Road, Leeds.

I was always proud of the fact that having sustained such a devastating calamity, we managed to retain full employment for all members of the factory staff. The full story was no doubt fully reported in the *Yorkshire Evening Post* at the time.

The manager of the Central Repairs Factory at the time of the fire was Harry Daubney (since deceased). My position at that time was Area Manager for the North of England and Ireland and it therefore became my responsibility to re-allocate the staff in such a manner that any inconvenience to our customers was kept to an absolute minimum. Happy days!

205 One of the Benefit Footwear branches in Birmingham after the Second World War.

206 Not all the Public Benefit Boot Company branches were on a grand scale. This photograph of the branch at 8 Stonegate Road, Leeds, was taken 11 November 1942. The Benefit sign stood out strongly in the wintry urban streetscape. Adjacent enterprises were J. Ellis & Company, boot repairs; Leeds Drug Company; Vennard's confectioners and the Meanwood Post Office.

There were some happy days, but also some not-so-happy days ahead as changing times and corporate manoeuvring buffeted the company.

The 1950s and 1960s brought enormous changes and challenges. The southern-based firm, Lilley and Skinner, acquired a major shareholding in Benefit Footwear, merged with Saxone and bought out Parker Shoes. Both Saxone and Parker were well-established and successful companies. The merging of these enterprises ushered in a new era and shops were refurbished to reflect this. Shoes were imported from Italy, France, Spain and Poland. Brand name shoes such as Brevit, Birthday, Airbourne, Norvic and Hush Puppies appeared in the Saxone, Lilley and Skinner, and the Benefit group of shops.

Olive Smeatham, who was still working for Benefit Footwear in the 1950s, reflected on the changing store environment:

> … no more fitting shoes, racks were used for display, customers were expected to choose from them. If a customer took too long in deciding, we were expected not to waste time, there was always another customer—modern times!

Sales techniques were changing in many footwear stores to self-service to accelerate sales. Another former employee, Mr Wiseman, recalls: 'Abbott and Clark tried the first self-service shop in around 1959 in Camden town I think, but they lost more stock than they sold.'

208 *Arthur Hudson who joined Benefit Footwear in 1947 and went on to a managerial role with the company. He subsequently became President of the National Association of Multiple Boot and Shoe Repairers.*

Things were moving fast within the footwear industry and competition was very keen. The main threat stemmed from the activities of Charles Clore who had recently acquired the Sears/Trueform group including Freeman Hardy and Willis. Clore had property interests but very quickly realised the potential in shoe retailing and went on to acquire the Manfield and Dolcis chain of stores, thereby adding hundreds of retail footwear outlets to his empire.

209 Typical Benefit Footwear store fascia of the early 1950s.

210 The Benefit Footwear premises in Uttoxeter in the 1950s. This was an era when window dressing developed as a more professional art form. Careful attention was paid to ensure that the display in each window looked elegant and appealing.

The fierce competition forced Lilley and Skinner on to the offensive and they took the decision to merge with Saxone, who held the well-respected trademarks known as Saxone, Cable and Sorosis. This alliance in 1956 brought together some 475 shops, four factories, 15 repair factories and six warehouses in the UK and Ireland. Additionally, the enterprise supported a worldwide export trade through retail branches in Canada and shoe factories in South Africa and Australia.

The next step was to form a holding company: Saxone, Lilley and Skinner Holdings, known rather indelicately by the acronym SLASH. The new holding company included Benefit Footwear, which in effect became a working subsidiary

of Lilley and Skinner. All of this meant a period of reorganisation and rationalisation. In the process, the Cable company, which owned branches in Scotland and operated in a similar way to Benefit Footwear, merged their operations with those of Benefit Footwear.

The decision to place the Cable and Benefit Footwear businesses together was made to extend and strengthen the companies' share in that sector of the market. This would have been strongly supported by Tom Eggleton, Managing Director of Benefit Footwear and a SLASH board member at the time.

Benefit Footwear closed down its old offices and moved to a purpose-built office complex on a disused industrial estate at Seacroft on the north-eastern outskirts of Leeds. The street that was once used to supply the pits, Coal Road, was upgraded to take light industrial and housing development. Apart from the head office for the Benefit and Cable companies, a brand new all-purpose warehouse and distribution centre was added to accommodate the needs, not only of Benefit and Cable, but also of Saxone, Lilley and Skinner. Previous distribution points in Kilmarnock, Northampton, Stockport and Leeds were scaled down and closed.

The new Seacroft site occupied 11 acres including the head office and it was capable of storing millions of pairs of shoes at any one time. It was very advanced for its time and highly mechanised, fulfilling and dispatching orders far more rapidly than had previously been achieved as well as radically reducing costs.

A company publication of the time, *Fleet of Foot*, enthusiastically describes the most noticeable feature of the new distribution complex—its mechanisation:

212 *The Public Benefit Boot Company commenced business in the ancient Market Place of Newark in the early 1890s. They moved to several locations in Market Place over the following years and finally settled next to the entrance to the noted* Clinton Arms Hotel. *The photograph shows the premises in the 1960s.*

213 *Saxone trademarks from the 1960s era.*

It is a very quiet place, where the sudden rattle of a stock truck on the latticed mezzanine floor breaks an almost cathedral calm, and where in the little group of essential offices the teleprinters' patter sounds improperly noisy. When an executive needs to be contacted in the warehouse a signal reaches him and him alone on a walkie-talkie receiver which he has slipped into his breast pocket on the way from his office. Even the girls who work in overalls and trouser in the stockroom walk in slippers whose flat heels will not catch in the lattice flooring of the upper storey and make scarcely a sound.

By this time, SLASH had reduced the number of branches to 500 and was ready to do battle with the giant British Shoe Corporation (BSC) which had around 1,500 branches.

A man who became very close to Charles Clore was Harry Levison. He was born into a shoe retailing family—his parents and later his brother operated shoe shops in London. Levison himself began as a travelling salesman before opening his first shoe shop in 1927 at Camden Town. Lilley and Skinner supplied him with stock for his outlets that were often located in market environments. Working on the principle of low profit margins—selling cheap but in vast quantities, his business quickly flourished. By 1940 he had 15 branches and had prospered sufficiently to open an office and warehouse in Fortess Road, Kentish Town and registered the new company name of Fortess Shoe Company.

By 1954 Levison had 39 branches and his success, due largely to his prudent no-waste no-nonsense management style, came to the attention of Charles Clore who was looking for opportunities to expand. Clore bought the Fortess Shoe Company and had Levison continue in a management role. The Fortess name was dropped and the name Curtess was adopted. The change entailed the alteration of just two letters on the store fascias—a fine example of Levison's economical style of thinking. Levison's valuable contribution and business experience was acknowledged when he was subsequently appointed managing director of True Form, FH&W and later Dolcis and Manfield.

The various units operating within SLASH suffered a severe financial setback in 1957–58 when Saxone, which had invested in Australia, lost heavily and considerably weakened the position of SLASH. Another blow came with the sudden death in 1959 of the SLASH chairman Thomas Lilley, rendering the company even more vulnerable to takeover bids, particularly as he had held the majority shareholding within the group.

Charles Clore continued to swallow up old established names in the footwear trade. When Thomas Lilley died, his substantial shareholding passed to his

216 Benefit Footwear window display of the 1960s. Window dressers were highly skilled individuals and they would often work from photographs of mock displays that had been set up at the head office. This ensured a more professional result and a degree of continuity in the presentation from branch to branch.

214 Cable Footwear window display of the 1960s.

215 Style of ladies shoe sold by Benefit Footwear in the 1950s and 1960s.

217 Part of the huge rationalisation programme in the 1960s saw Benefit Footwear and Cables Shoes set up at their new headquarter at Seacroft, Leeds.

218 Saxone delivery vans that looked a little like shoeboxes themselves were once a familiar sight on British roads.

219 The BSC warehouse at Braunstone.

220 Opposite: The entities that made up the British Shoe Corporation in 1962, compiled from text prepared by Bruce Robinson during his time as Assistant Managing Director of BSC.

wife and family and by 1962 Charles Clore had managed to acquire a substantial part of that shareholding in SLASH. From then on Benefit shops were under a real threat as Clore and the British Shoe Corporation embarked on a programme of rationalisation in an attempt to eliminate over-representation in some areas.

BSC was to be run as a centralised corporation and a head office and extensive distribution complex were built at Braunstone, Leicester. The city of Leicester was chosen for a number of reasons; it was in the heart of the shoe manufacturing region, it was in the middle of the country and it had good motorway access. Another major influence was the fact that the largest of the BSC divisions, FH&W, was already operating from Leicester and could provide appropriate infrastructure.

The companies forming BSC started moving into the new headquarters in December 1963. The various offices and warehouses throughout the country were closed and all administration and distribution was concentrated at Braunstone. The warehouse, with additions completed in 1967 and 1982, had a floor area of more than one million square feet. It was claimed to be the largest single-storey warehouse in Europe with racks that held up to 10 million pairs of shoes. The warehouse operated on a 24-hour basis six days a week with a staff of 750 people.

The Seacroft premises of Benefit and SLASH were closed and everything transferred to the new BSC site at Braunstone. Benefit operated in name only as they awaited their fate from BSC.

BENEFIT with head office and warehouse in Leeds. First branch opened in 1875 by William Franklin in Hull. By the turn of the century the Public Benefit Boot and Shoe Company had 100 branches throughout the country.

CURTESS with head office and warehouse in London. Commenced 1927 when Harry Levison opened his first shoe shop in London. 1940 became Fortess Shoe Company Limited with 15 branches. 1954 had 39 branches when it became part of the Sears Holdings Limited and changed its name to Curtess Shoes Limited. Moved to the BSC complex at Braunstone in 1964. In the 1980s Curtess had 300 branches all over the UK.

DOLCIS with head office and warehouse in London. In 1865 John Upson started selling shoes from a street barrow at Woolwich Market. Business continued by his son John Upson. Upsons Limited became a private company in 1914. Traded under the name of Dolcis from 1920. Had a dominant position in the women's fashion market. Became a division of BSC in 1956.

FREEMAN HARDY & WILLIS with head office and warehouse in Leicester. In 1870 Edward Wood began manufacturing boots and shoes in Leicester. Six years later his company was incorporated and took on the name Freeman Hardy and Willis Limited (FH&W). In 1881 there were 40 branches and by 1926 there were 520 branches. Head office and warehouse in Rutland St, Leicester destroyed by fire after enemy bombing in 1940 with 750,000 pairs of shoes lost. 1953 Charles Clore acquired a majority shareholding of J Sears and became Chairman of FH&W. 1956 amalgamation of FH&W, Trueform, Curtess and Character Shoes to form BSC.

LILLEY & SKINNER with head office and warehouse in London. Commenced in 1825 in London by Thomas Lilley, continued by son Thomas Lilley ll who formed a partnership with W Banks Skinner in 1881. Private company Lilley & Skinner formed in 1894. After WW2 acquired a major shareholding in Benefit Shoe Company

SAXONE with head office and warehouse in Kilmarnock. In 1783 George Clark set up his trade as a shoemaker in Kilmarnock, Scotland. His sons developed the business and with major expansion in Brazil. Links were forged with F & G Abbott Limited and in 1908 they merged with the Clark & Son to form Saxone Shoe Company. In 1950 Saxone launched the first challenge to Dolcis, in the heartland of their business, opening at 297 Oxford Street, followed by further branches at Marble Arch and the Strand. 1956 with Lilley & Skinner under a London based holding company SLS Holdings (SLASH), while the operating companies kept their existing boards. Early rationalisation involved transferring most of the Cable branches to Benefit Footwear, a Lilley & Skinner subsidiary, which traded in a like grade. 1962 Saxone, Lilley & Skinner became a division of BSC.

TRUEFORM with head office and warehouse in Northampton. Founded in 1891 by J G Sears and went public as J Sears (True-Form) Boot Company Limited in 1912. In 1929 acquired the controlling interest in Freeman Hardy & Willis in what was the biggest transaction of its kind in the shoe trade history. Just after the war the joint company (True-Form and Freeman Hardy & Willis) had 855 shops. In 1953 the company was taken over by Charles Clore to form the nucleus of BSC. In 1954 True-Form was sold to Freeman Hardy & Willis and FH&W subsequently changed its name to British Shoe Corporation.

BSC

BRITISH SHOE CORPORATION

Over the nine years 1953–1962 BSC emerged as an amalgamation of Benefit Footwear and six other major footwear enterprises.

221 In the latter years of Benefit Footwear, repairs were transferred to small shop units in various locations. The last repair shop, at 33 Queen Victoria Street in Leeds, closed in 1986. Here, Benefit Footwear employees gather happily outside the Queen Victoria Street repair shop in the early 1980s.

The BSC empire now consisted of Dolcis, FH&W, Trueform, Curtess and Manfield, as well as the SLASH group. The criteria for the redistribution of Benefit shops appeared to follow a pattern: if a Benefit shop was in a city market area it would transfer to Curtess—the keen-price chain. If a Benefit shop traded in Harrogate or Knaresborough, for example, it transferred to Manfield or FH&W as those towns were for family shopping. The Benefit shop in Scarborough became Saxone.

Charles Clore began to see that shopping trends were changing with the development of new, large shopping centres and out-of-town centres. Former prime sites were quickly becoming secondary sites. The companies that achieved the higher returns (which also turned out to be the big boys of the shoe world—Saxone, FH&W and Curtess), were transferred to the new shopping precincts. During this takeover period Manfield absorbed a high proportion of Benefit and Cable branches, and BSC sold surplus sites for a handsome profit.

There are two views regarding the possible fate that awaited Benefit Footwear. One is that by joining the SLASH group they gave themselves the best possible chance of survival. The group had centralised their entire operations in a state-of-the-art office, distribution and warehousing complex. The group's branches had been rationalised and wastage had been severely reduced. However, fate took a bad turn when heavy losses in Australia and the untimely death of Thomas Lilley left them in a vulnerable position.

Mr Bruce Robinson, former Assistant Managing Director of BSC, put forward another view – that Benefit Footwear may have survived and prospered had it been more progressive or pro-active in expanding after the Second World War and if it had not joined SLASH. Whilst joining SLASH may have appeared the best move at the time, with hindsight it may have been a hasty decision made in a period of extreme pressure.

BSC, which used to account for around 20 per cent of the UK footwear market, collapsed dramatically in 1997. The former BSC retail outlets continued under different ownership; chains such as Shoe Express, Dolcis and Saxone continued under their new owners.

Similar fates awaited the two Lennard family companies as they succumbed to the massive manoeuvring and takeover activity in the footwear trade.

The Bristol-based Lennards Limited continued operating independently but by the late 1970s investment groups bought into the company. The Great Universal Stores became a holding company for Lennards Limited and in 1981 a substantial re-fitting of their stores took place. They continued operating under the Lennards Limited name until 1988 when the decision was made to cease the company's retail trading.

Lennards Brothers in Leicester over the years had changed their name to Liberty Shoes and then to Tandem Shoes but by 1992 they went into administrative

222 From early in the 20th century Public Benefit occupied premises at 82 Shields Road and for the following decades operated four branches in Newcastle-on-Tyne for much of the time. The view shows Northumberland Street where the company had a branch at number 40 from 1935 until 1968.

223 In the 1950s Lennards continued to occupy a commanding corner site at The Cross, Worcester.

224 *Two of the major players in the final years of the Benefit Footwear story are evident in this view of Market Place, Wigan. On the left is a Cable store and, on the other side of Market Place, Benefit Footwear competes for business. This situation ended a few short years later when these two companies merged under a rationalisation programme.*

225 *The company had a major presence in Birmingham on the corner of Corporation Street and Union Street for close to 100 years. In the 1880s under the management of Benjamin Hunn, they traded as The Public Benefit Boot Company and in the 1980s they were still there under the Lennards' name. This 1975 view of the premises also shows the City Arcade on Union Street that was built in the early 1900s to an art nouveau design.*

receivership. Around 23 of their outlets were taken over by Stead and Simpson and 45 were bought by Shoefayre – the latter being one of the few multiple footwear retailers still operating in the early part of the 21st century.

The vision and dreams of the Franklin, Lennard and related families had survived for more than a hundred years.

7 Epilogue

Looking back at the first 25 or 30 years of the Public Benefit business activities, one has to ask the question—how was it possible to achieve so much in so little time? Certainly the confidence and unbridled optimism at the time were significant factors but so too were the personal qualities, strong work ethic and social attitudes that were so much a part of the Victorian era.

Many of the Public Benefit partners, directors and managers appear to have led unpretentious lifestyles for many years as they worked long and hard to build up the business. Each partner concentrated on establishing a good reputation and expanding the company name and they avoided the temptation to reward themselves with huge salaries or lavish lifestyles. The grand houses and other rewards came later—for many years it appears that all profits were turned back into further development of the business.

Some of the Public Benefit directors entered politics: perhaps most notable was the Chairman, James T. Woodhouse (later Sir James) who became the Liberal MP for West Hull and went on to become Lord Mayor of Hull and finally Liberal MP for Huddersfield.

Brow Dickinson was elected as a Liberal councillor in Leeds and held the post for many years. Something of Brow Dickinson's personal qualities and his role in the development of the Public Benefit business can be gleaned from

226 There are numerous reminders of the company's presence in cities and towns throughout the country. Many of their substantial buildings still stand including this one on Holderness Road, Hull, where the decorative boot motif remains evident.

227 The company trademark and slogan 'Wear guaranteed. Over a quarter of a century's reputation' featured on various forms of early advertising. Items such as this company enamel advertising sign are now highly sought after by collectors.

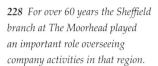

228 *For over 60 years the Sheffield branch at The Moorhead played an important role overseeing company activities in that region.*

229 *Brow Dickinson (1857–1931)*

230 *William Henry Franklin (1848–1907)*

the following article that appeared in the *Yorkshire Observer* of 6 November 1924:

Yorkshire Grit

Mr Dickinson's romantic career began over forty years ago at Bramley, Leeds, when along with two brothers he commenced, in just a willy-nilly sort of way, be it said, to manufacture boots by hand, in a tiny room in the house of their parents.

Clouds lay thick over the modest enterprise of these three lads, and many times sad disappointments sapped away their spirits, but that indefinable something known to most of us as faith spurred them on through desperate odds, and bit by bit the silver lining gradually appeared upon the horizon.

A Lucky Venture

After building up a fairly big connection—only achieved through hard and unremitting toil—the three brothers, in the year 1897, joined up with six other firms which eventually became known throughout the country as the Leeds Public Benefit Boot Company, which today owns 150 retail shops, not to mention the spacious factory in Park Square, Leeds, where the whole of the firm's products are manufactured.

And throughout the many prosperous years the firm has been in existence, the chief dynamic force of the latter has been Mr Brow Dickinson. Possessed of tact, personality, and a happy prescience of what is essential in business, social, and, last but not least, municipal affairs, Mr Dickinson stands today pre-eminent as the best type of Yorkshireman.

In fact, the latter's achievements demonstrate to the full that the sweets of life are denied no man who cares to go to the trouble to fight for them.

William Franklin's parents and his extended family were closely involved in the enterprise, particularly in the early years of the company. His mother Eunice died at 13 Stanley Street, Hull in 1882 and his father Richard died whilst managing the Grantham shop in 1889.

In the early 1880s, when William was in his mid-30's, he married Ellen Sarbutt and they had three children. By the 1890s William Franklin had moved into a house in fashionable Park Street, Hull. He later moved to a residence—Linden

House in Pearson Park, Hull (known as The Park at the time), and finally settled in a large house named Cherry Garth in Cottingham. In February 1905 William Franklin resigned as a director of the Public Benefit Boot Company and he died in August 1907 at the age of sixty-one. Two children predeceased him—his only son Willie died aged 11 months and a daughter Ethel died in 1906 aged 22 years. Hilda, the one surviving daughter, married a Hull solicitor, Oscar Mackrill, in 1912.

232 George Edward Franklin (1849–1913)

233 The exterior of George Franklin's mansion in Osmaston Road, Derby. Set in generous grounds, the home included a music room, smoking room, breakfast room, drawing room, coach-house, marble stables, office block, billiard room, conservatory and maids' quarters.

William's brother, George Edward Franklin, married Elizabeth Hunn in Grimsby in 1872. There were five children from this marriage and a further three children from a second relationship. George, like the other directors, initially lived above his Public Benefit premises at 24–28 London Road, Derby. In 1895 he was living in a modest house at 132 Osmaston Road and shortly afterwards he moved into a grand Regency-style villa named The Field at 237 Osmaston Road, Derby. This large home stood on the east side of Osmaston Road by Bloomfield Street from around 1820 until at least 1971.

234 *Sumptuous interior of George Franklin's mansion in 1908 with much evidence of his penchant for collecting works of art and fine furnishings.*

235 *One of George Franklin's prize-winning brood mares, 'Lady Denmark Gobang'.*

236 *Medal won by George Franklin in 1905 at the Hackney Horse Society show at Heanor for his entry 'Little Prudence'*

George was an accomplished organist and, installed in his mansion, was a fine organ made by Binns of Bramley. He served as a Derby City councillor and he also took an interest in breeding and training horses including the renowned 'Lord Gobang' and 'Lady Gobang'. He won several thousand pounds in the leading shows of the day including, London, Royal, Richmond and the Royal Agricultural Show.

George Franklin resigned as a director of the Public Benefit Boot Company in March 1906 and two years later he auctioned the contents of The Field prior to moving to Hadleigh in the south of England. George's opulent lifestyle can be gauged from the 1908 auction catalogue that illustrated and described many fine paintings, sculpture and antiques. He died in Hadleigh in 1913 aged 64 and was survived by eight of his ten children.

237 *George Franklin's mansion contained a rich and large collection of items including a full-size Thurston billiard table, several organs, a concert grand piano, an elaborate gilt bronze clock, Chippendale bedroom suites, oak dining room appointments, paintings by Murillo and Turner, marble and bronze statuary and candelabras that were formerly the property of Queen Isabella of Spain.*

238 *George Franklin and his wife Elizabeth stand third and fourth from the left on the marriage of their son Horace Franklin to Rosetta Burdett Turner on 7 June 1904 at Newark.*

Descendants of the Franklins are today widely scattered around the world—in the USA, Canada, South Africa, Zimbabwe, Australia, England and Belgium. Many of them look with a degree of awe and respect at the role their forebears played in the remarkable story of the Public Benefit Boot Company—a story that was the talk of the trade for many decades.

Bibliography

Benefit Footwear Limited, *Benefit Footwear Limited 1897-1947; A brief history* (Leeds, 1947)

Briscoe, J. Potter, *Nottinghamshire and Derbyshire at the opening of the twentieth century: Contemporary biographies* (Pike's New Century Series, ed. W. Pike, W.T. Pike, Brighton, 1901)

Bristol: An alphabetically arranged guide to the industrial resources of the ancient Royal and free city – leading merchants and manufacturers of Bristol and Bath (Birmingham, 1888)

Building News, vol xxxvi, 17 Jan 1879

Carr, E. T., *Industry in Bramley* (Leeds, 1938)

Clark, Alan, *Elton: A history of the lost and ancient buildings of this Northampton village* (Spiegl, Stamford, 1992)

Gordon, Colin, *By gaslight in winter* (Hamish Hamilton, London, 1980)

Lennards Limited, *Lennards: Britain's best bootmakers* (Bristol, 1929)

Linstrum, Derek, *Historic architecture of Leeds* (Oriel, Newcastle upon Tyne, 1969)

Pike, W. T. (ed.) *Bristol in 1898-99: Contemporary biographies* (W. T. Pike, Brighton, 1899)

Price, Stephen J., *Birmingham old and new* (E. P. Publishing, Wakefield, 1976)

'Public Benefit Boot Co., Ltd.', *Illustrated Hull* (1898) pp. 40-1

Saxone and Lilley & Skinner, *Fleet of Foot: The headquarters of Benefit and Cable Shoes and distribution centre for the Saxone and Lilley & Skinner group of companies* (Leeds, 1960)

Sheeran, George, *Leeds: The architectural heritage* (Ryburn, Halifax, 1993)

Shoe & Leather Record, 17 August 1917, p.155

'St Paul's House', *Journal of the Victorian Society – West Yorkshire*, vol 8 (1988)

Swann, June, *Shoemaking* (Shire, Aylesbury, 1986)

'The Public Benefit Boot Co., Ltd., Leeds.', *Shoe & Leather News Biographical Directory of Great Britain (Supplement)*, 29 Mar 1917, pp. iv-v

Vickers, Harold, *A guide to Beverley containing a map of the district, 13 pictures and descriptive letterpress, being number 239 of The Borough Guides* (Edward J. Burrow, Royal Publishing Office, Cheltenham, c.1907)

Warne, F. G. (ed.), 1913, *Bristol 1913: Its history, its commerce, its citizens – an album de luxe* (Rankin, Bristol, 1913)

'Yorkshire grit', *Yorkshire Observer*, 6 November 1924

Subscribers

ALBEMARLE RESIDENTIAL HOME
JAN BAILEY
ANTHONY L BEAN
BARBARA BEAN
GERALDINE L BEAN
MICHAEL D BEAN
ROBERT A BEAN
(MISS) GERAL F C BILLINGHURST
DIANNE & TERRY BLACK (CUZDX2)
CHRIS & SHIRLEY BONNETT
PETER BROADBERRY—BROADBERRY SHOES
DAVID BROUGHTON
A W BROWN
D MICHAEL BROWN
P F & S A BRYCE
PAULINE BURKE (NÉE TURNER)
CHARLES & MADELINE CAROME
HELEN CAFFELLE CASTONGUAY
R I CAWKWELL
CORNWALL CENTRE, REDRUTH
COURTNEY LIBRARY, ROYAL INSTITUTION OF
    CORNWALL
JOHN CRAVEN
PETER J DRAKES
MRS MYRA DRAYTON
RESIDENTS OF ELM TREE COURT, HULL
STEPHEN ETHERIDGE
JOHN EVANS
FOOTSHOP LTD T/A COSYFEET—HIP TO TOE
CHRISTOPHER PAUL FRANKLIN
MARJORIE D FRANKLIN
MICHAEL GEORGE EDWARD FRANKLIN
PETER FRANKLIN
RICHARD TONY FRANKLIN
V J for GEORGE FRANKLIN
(MRS P W) FRIEDA MARY FRANKLIN-BILLINGHURST
PAUL L GIBSON
JOHN GILLEGHAN MBE
JUDITH A HAGEN
MAURICE HARRAND
WILLIAM HERRENDEN-HARKER
HICA LTD
MICHAEL C HINDLE
MR A R HUDSON
RAYMOND HYLAND
CLIVE JACKSON
CAROLYNE & HAROLD KELLEY
KINGSTON UPON HULL LIBRARIES

CAROLINE LEWIS
ENID & IAN LOCKE
DAVID LOCKYER
J DAVID LOVERING
W JOHN LOVERING
WALTER J LOVERING
ANTHONY MICHAEL MACKRILL
CHRISTOPHER ANTHONY MACKRILL
IAN MACKRILL
MICHAEL FRANKLIN MACKRILL
PETER OSCAR MACKRIL
IRIS MADDEN
VAL MARTIN-WARREN
PAUL & SALLY MCWATTERS
ROD NASH
MR PETER J NEWMAN MBE
NORTHAMPTON MUSEUM & ART GALLERY
DOREEN & TERRY OWEN
PLYMOUTH LIBRARY SERVICES
MR T PURKIS
ROSALIE RAINE
PATRICIA SANSAM
DUSTY & GILL SAUNDERS
DOLCE JEAN FRANKLIN SCHELL
MARILYN SCHELL
GLENN SEAGER
BILL SEDDON
BRUCE SEDDON
LORNA SEDDON
MICHAEL SEDDON
ROBERT GEORGE SEDDON
ROGER SEDDON
STEPHEN SEDDON
IAN SHIELDS
MALCOLM SHIELDS
SHEILA SIMPSON
MARIE MULLENNEIX SPEARMAN
ELIZABETH THACKER
SUE THACKER
J C B TURNER
PAT & JOHN TURNER
JILL TYDEMAN
KATHLEEN SYLVIA TYDEMAN
MRS MAISIE WAGGOTT
WAKEFIELD LIBRARIES & INFORMATION SERVICES
CLIFF & JUNE WHITEHOUSE
HARVEY WILLIS
WILLIAM M WISEMAN—ADM FOR BSC FOOTWEAR

Index